Preschool Patterns
EARLY LEARNING TIMESAVERS

by Marilynn G. Barr

Publisher: Roberta Suid
Editor: Carol Whiteley

Entire contents copyright © 1990
by Monday Morning Books, Inc., Box 1680,
Palo Alto, California 94302

Monday Morning is a registered trademark of Monday Morning Books, Inc.

Permission is hereby granted to the individual purchaser
to reproduce student materials in this book for non-commercial
individual or classroom use only. Permission is not granted
for school-wide or system-wide reproduction of materials.

ISBN 1-878279-20-3
Printed in the United States of America
9 8 7 6 5 4 3 2

For a complete catalog,
write to the address above.

Table of Contents

Introduction	5
Craft and Gift Ideas	6
Character of the Day	
Teddy Bear	7
Mouse	8
Elephant	9
Butterfly	10
Whale	11
Headband Strips	
Letters and Numbers	12
Color Words and Shapes	13
Halloween	14
Thanksgiving	15
Christmas	16
Valentine's Day	17
Spring	18
Stick Puppet Characters	
Nursery Rhyme Patterns	
Mother Goose and Mouse	19
Tub and Butcher	20
Baker and Candlestick Maker	21
Cat and Dog	22
Cow and Lamb	23
Miss Muffet and Jack Horner	24
Mother Hubbard and Old King Cole	25
Moon, Dish, and Spoon	26
Bottle of Bubbles and Pipe	27
Bowl, Fiddle, and Spider	28
Children	
Caucasian Children	29
African American Children	30
Asian American Children	31
Name Tags	
School Bell	32
Heart	33
Rainbow	34
Bunny	35
Field Trip	36
Badges	
I Can Tie!	37
I Can Lace!	38
I Can Count to 10	39
I Can. . . (Open)	40
Cubby Hole Labels	
Fall	41
Winter	42
Spring	43
Summer	44
Desk Labels	
Fall	45
Winter	46
Spring	47
Summer	48
Activity Center Labels	
Music	49
Traffic Safety	50
Reading	51
Arts and Crafts	52
Building Blocks	53
Outline Activity Patterns	
Cat	54
Dog	55
Elephant	56
Hippopotamus	57
Pig	58

Outline Activity Patterns (continued)

Snail	59
Teddy Bear	60
Turtle	61
Acorn	62
Snowflake	63
Umbrella	64
Sailboat	65

Outline Holiday Patterns

Bunny	66
Basket	67
Heart	68
Pumpkin	69
Ghost	70
Turkey	71
Stocking	72
Menorah	73

Birthday Patterns

Name Tags	74
Candles	75
Headband Strips	76
Attendance Tags	77

Attendance Tags

Snowman and Hat	78
Basket and Egg	79
Flowerpot and Flower	80
Teddy Bear and Bow Tie	81

Doorknob Hangers

Gone for a Walk	82
Gone to the Library	83
Gone on a Field Trip	84
Resting	85
We're Having a Party	86

Open Calendars

Teacher Calendar	87
Student Calendar	88
Student Calendar Caps	90
Student Calendar Event Stickers	102
Student Calendar Weather Stickers	103

Activity Posters

Let's Go Shopping	104
What's Cooking?	105
When I Grow Up. . .	106

Clips Collections

Fall	107
Winter	110
Spring	113
Summer	116

Let's Play Dress Up

Astronaut	119
Farmer	120
Magician	121

Teacher Notes

(_____) Knows His/Her Numbers	122
(_____) Knows His/Her Colors	123
(_____) Knows His/Her Shapes	124
(_____) Knows His/Her Alphabet	125
We Are Learning. . .	126
We Need Your Help	127
Thank You	128

INTRODUCTION

Preschool Patterns includes a wide variety of patterns you can use in your classroom throughout the year. Turn them into stick puppets, use them as ornaments or for gifts, label cubby holes and learning areas with them—there are so many ways to work with these creative materials..

How to Use The Patterns

Character of the Day
Brighten up the school day with one of these large character patterns. Use the patterns to spruce up a classroom display or simply as stick puppets. You can also reproduce them to make into flannel board puppet characters, greeting cards, or to use with art activities.

Headband Strips
After children color headbands, they can wear them during skills practice, to greet a new season, or during holiday celebrations. Link them in chains to decorate the classroom or use them to frame paper crafts and/or art activities.

Stick Puppet Characters
Children will enjoy reciting Mother Goose rhymes with these characters and props.

Name Tags
These easy-to-color name tags can be used to identify classroom helpers or guest speakers or during Open House. Children will also enjoy decorating these patterns with buttons, cotton balls, beads, beans, and other craft materials to turn them into ornaments and gifts.

Badges
Being recognized and rewarded for achievement is important to children of all ages. As students learn to tie, lace, and count, reward them with a badge.

Cubby Hole and Desk Labels
Greet each season with new cubby hole and desk labels. The cubby hole patterns can also double as name tags or book labels. Have children color desk labels to glue to the front of work folders or to glue one to the bottom half of a sheet of construction paper that can be folded to make a greeting card.

Activity Center Labels
Make your activity centers clearly visible with these center labels. Children can also make their own activity scrapbooks. Example: Use the Music label for the cover. Have children cut pictures from magazines of musical instruments, people dancing, etc., to glue on pages in their booklet.

Outline Activity and Holiday Patterns
These bold outline patterns can be glued to the front of work folders. Wallpaper scraps will add instant color or children can customize their patterns with construction paper, colored tissue paper, and a variety of craft supplies. The patterns can also be hole-punched and glued to oaktag to make lace-up cards.

Birthday Patterns
Name tag, candle, and headband strip patterns are all you need to have a classroom birthday celebration. Attach the appropriate candle pattern to the front of a completed headband for the birthday boy or girl to wear during the festivities.

Attendance Tags
After each child has colored a tag, post the large tags along the bottom edge of a bulletin board, on either side of a door frame, or on a flannel board or wall. Using cuphooks, pushpins, or Velcro, students can attach their smaller tags for an easy-to-see attendance chart or to identify classroom helpers, the student of the week, and so on.

Doorknob Hangers
Use these doorknob hangers to let others know what your class is doing. You can also white out the message so children can write their own messages, then color and decorate the hangers for use at home or as gifts.

Activity Posters
After each child has colored the poster, have children glue pictures cut from magazines, greeting cards, or newspaper sale pages. For example, the "What's Cooking?" poster can help you teach about the four food groups; children can cut out and glue on pictures of fruits, vegetables, meats, and breads.

Open Calendars
The Student Open Calendar is designed to teach about the days of the week. It includes two spaces per day in which children can glue weather or special events stickers. Use a different calendar cap for each month.

Clips Collections
Here is a wonderful reference library of illustrations you can duplicate or enlarge for classroom displays, decorative art on worksheets, and to turn into gifts.

Let's Play Dress Up
Provide the children with the dress-up pattern they choose and let the fun begin! Teach the students songs, rhymes, and/or stories to go along with their dress-up costumes, and encourage them to create stories of their own.

Teacher Notes
Keeping open the lines of communication between home and school is a little easier with these take-home note forms that cover achievement, progress, requests for volunteers, and thank you's.

Craft and Gift Ideas

This section provides you with directions and diagrams for six different projects:

Greeting Cards

The children can decorate these with characters and headband strips.

Doorknob Hangers

Let students decorate these with the Mother Goose characters and a variety of craft materials.

Picture Frames

Use the headband strips and outline patterns and have the children decorate their frames with craft supplies.

Refrigerator Magnets

Using name tags and magnetic tape, children can either mount the patterns on construction paper squares or laminate them and mount the magnetic tape directly on the back. (For durability, have children mount the magnetic tape prior to laminating.)

Gift Tags

Have children color and cut out art from the seasonal Clips Collection to make gift tags. Paste onto small pieces of construction paper or oaktag. Punch holes and add yarn to finish each gift tag.

Character of the Day
Teddy Bear

7

Character of the Day
Mouse

Character of the Day
Elephant

Character of the Day
Butterfly

Character of the Day
Whale

11

Headband Strips
Letters and Numbers

Headband Strips
Color Words and Shapes

Headband Strips
Halloween

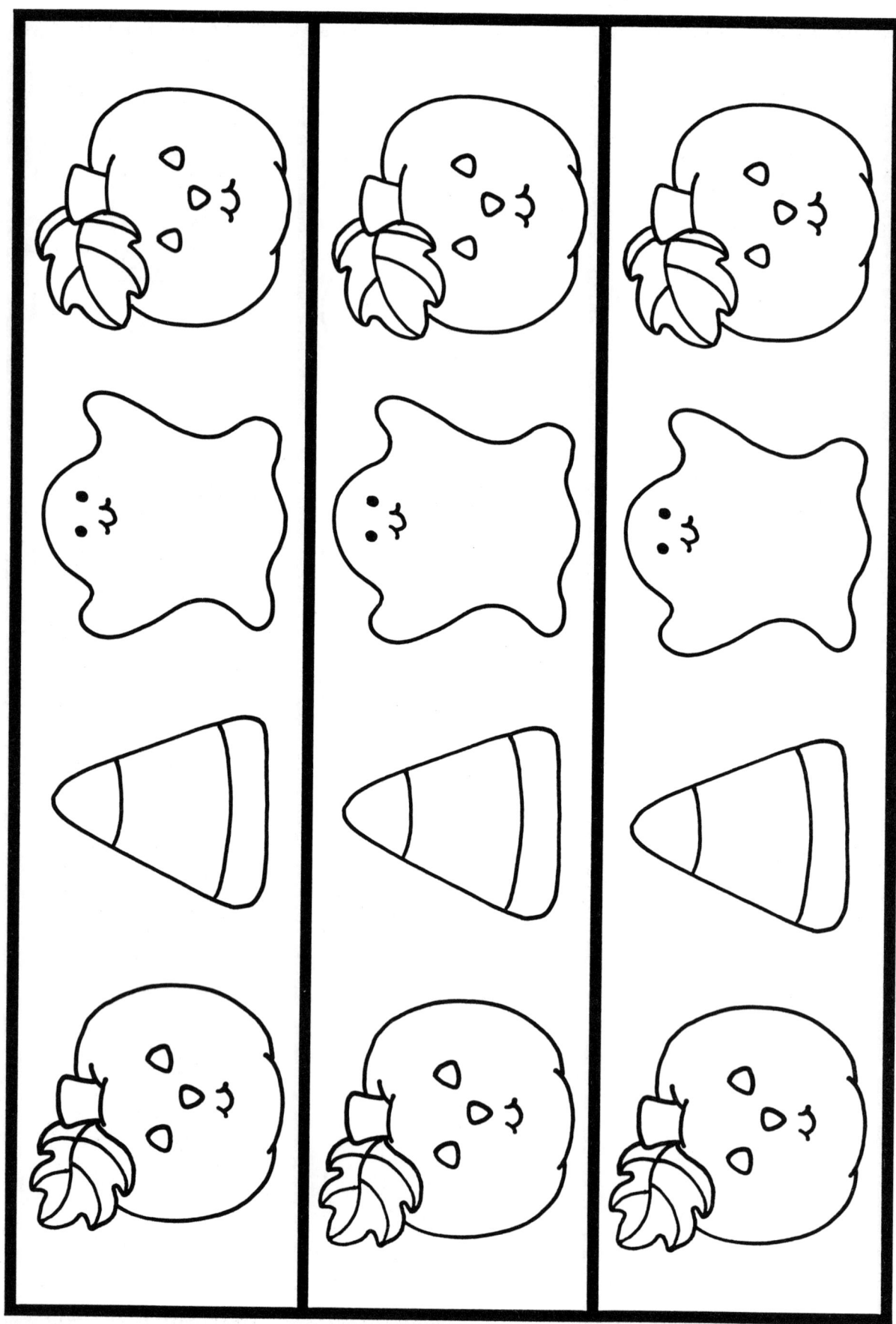

Headband Strips
Thanksgiving

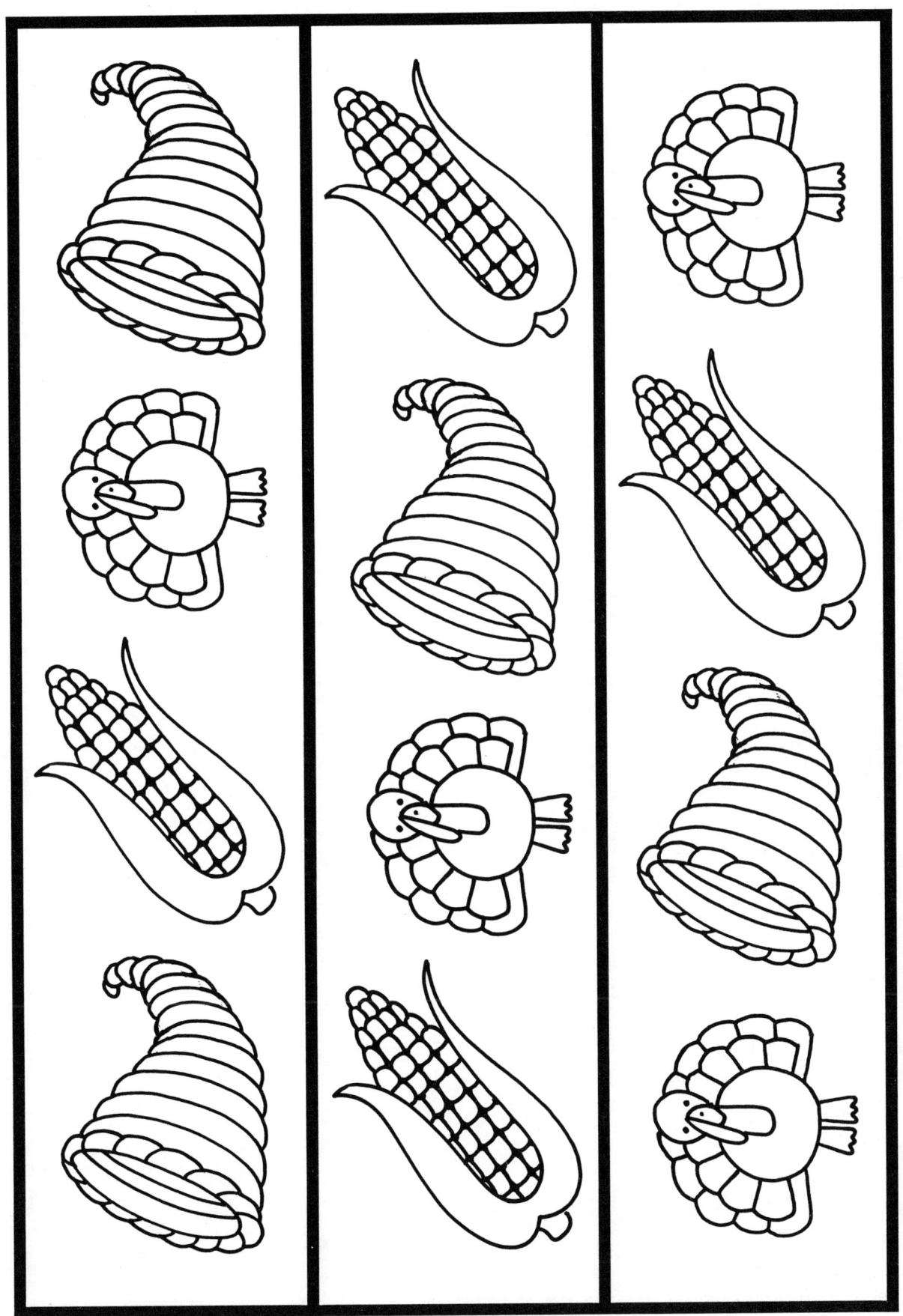

15

Headband Strips
Christmas

Headband Strips
Valentine's Day

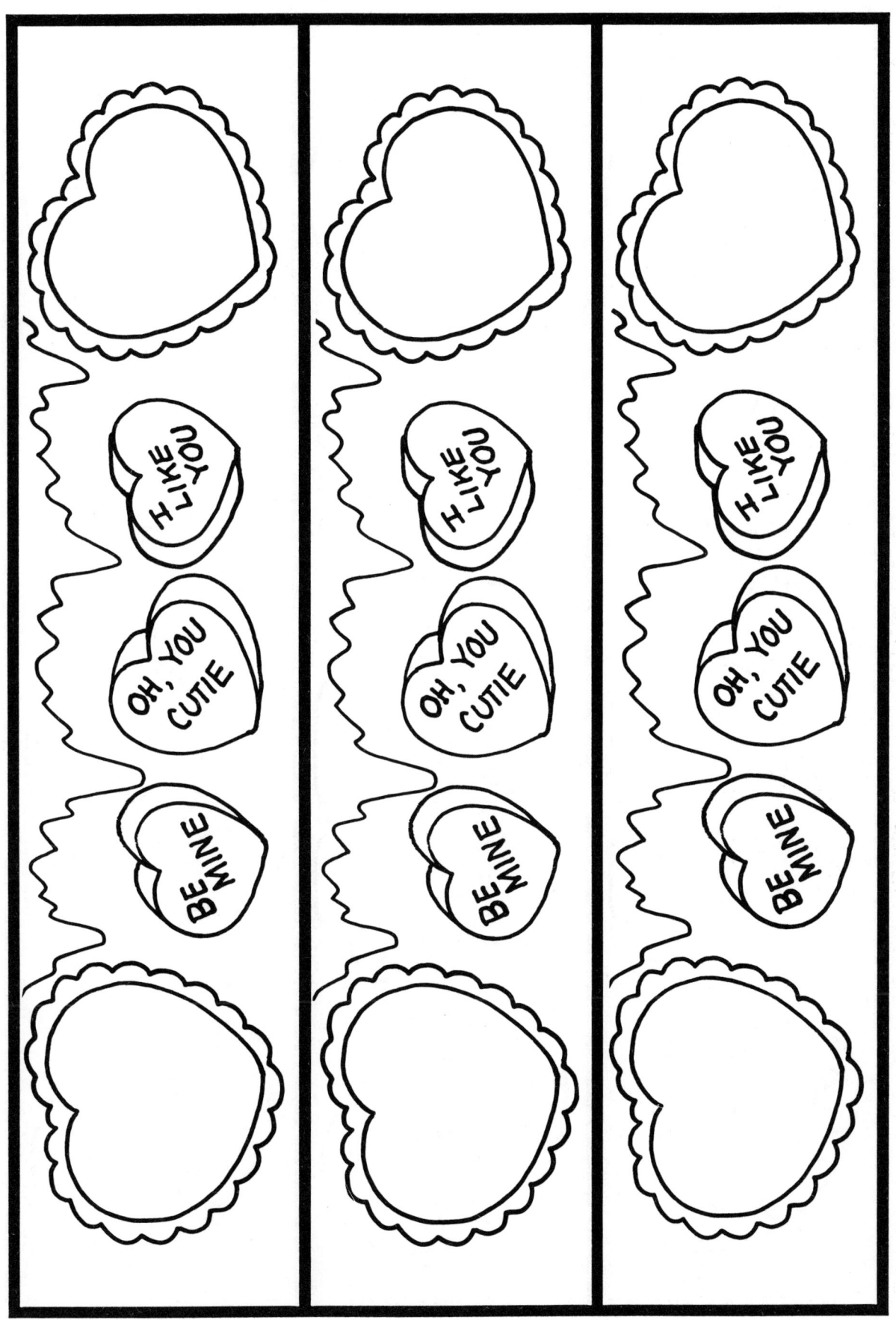

17

Headband Strips
Spring

Stick Puppet Patterns
Mother Goose and Mouse

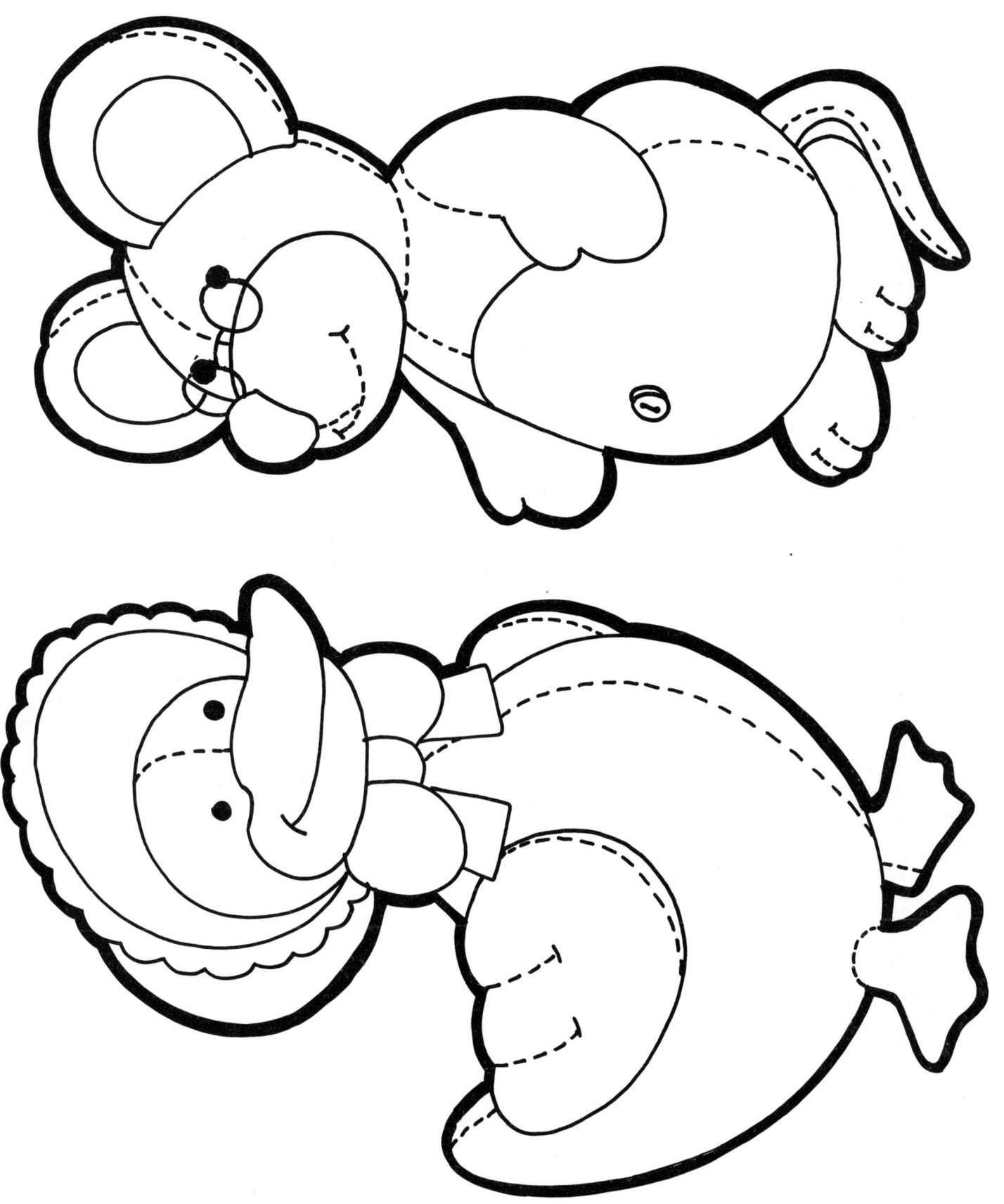

Stick Puppet Patterns
Tub and Butcher

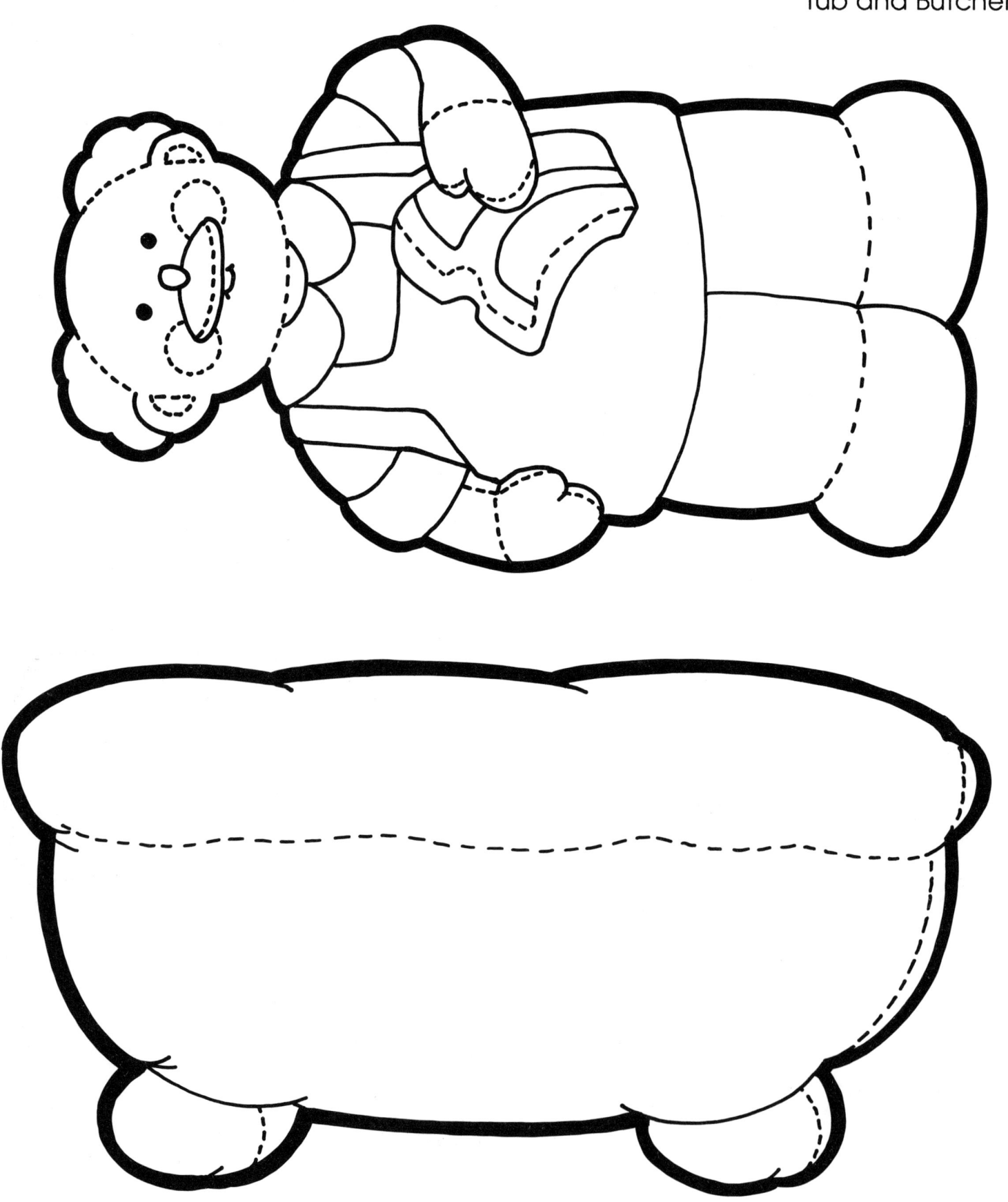

Stick Puppet Patterns
Baker and Candlestick Maker

Stick Puppet Patterns
Cat and Dog

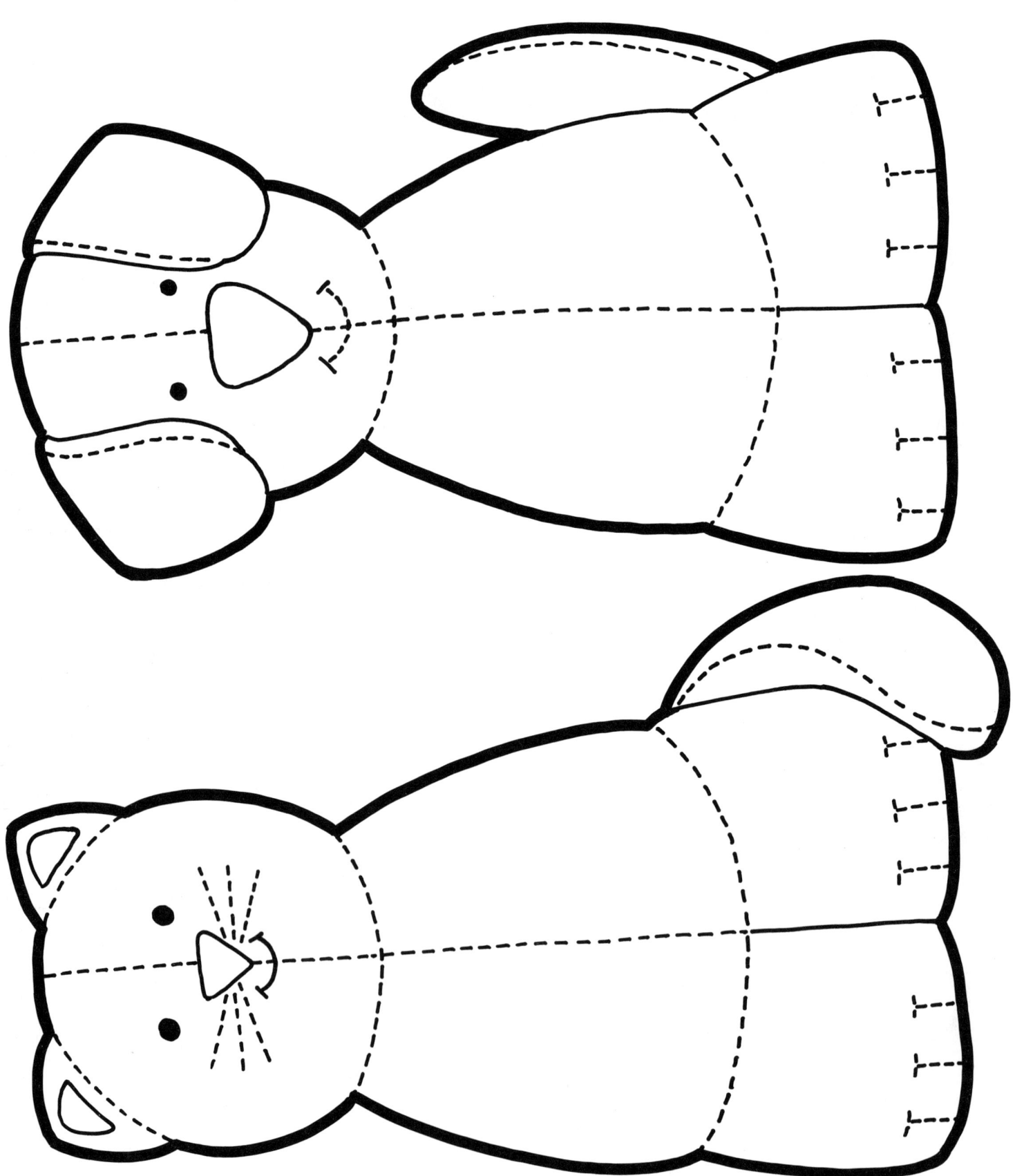

Stick Puppet Patterns
Cow and Lamb

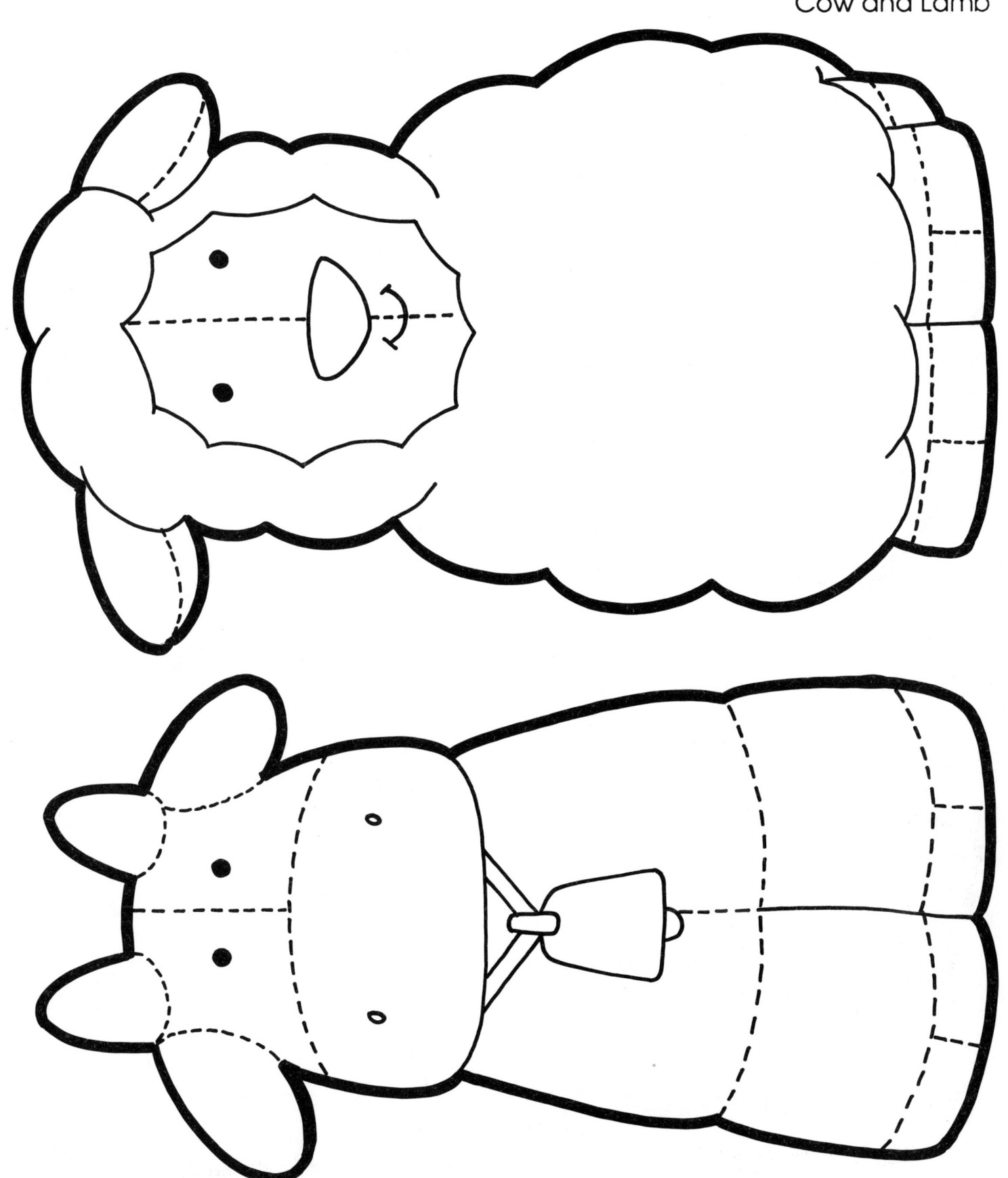

Stick Puppet Patterns
Miss Muffet and Jack Horner

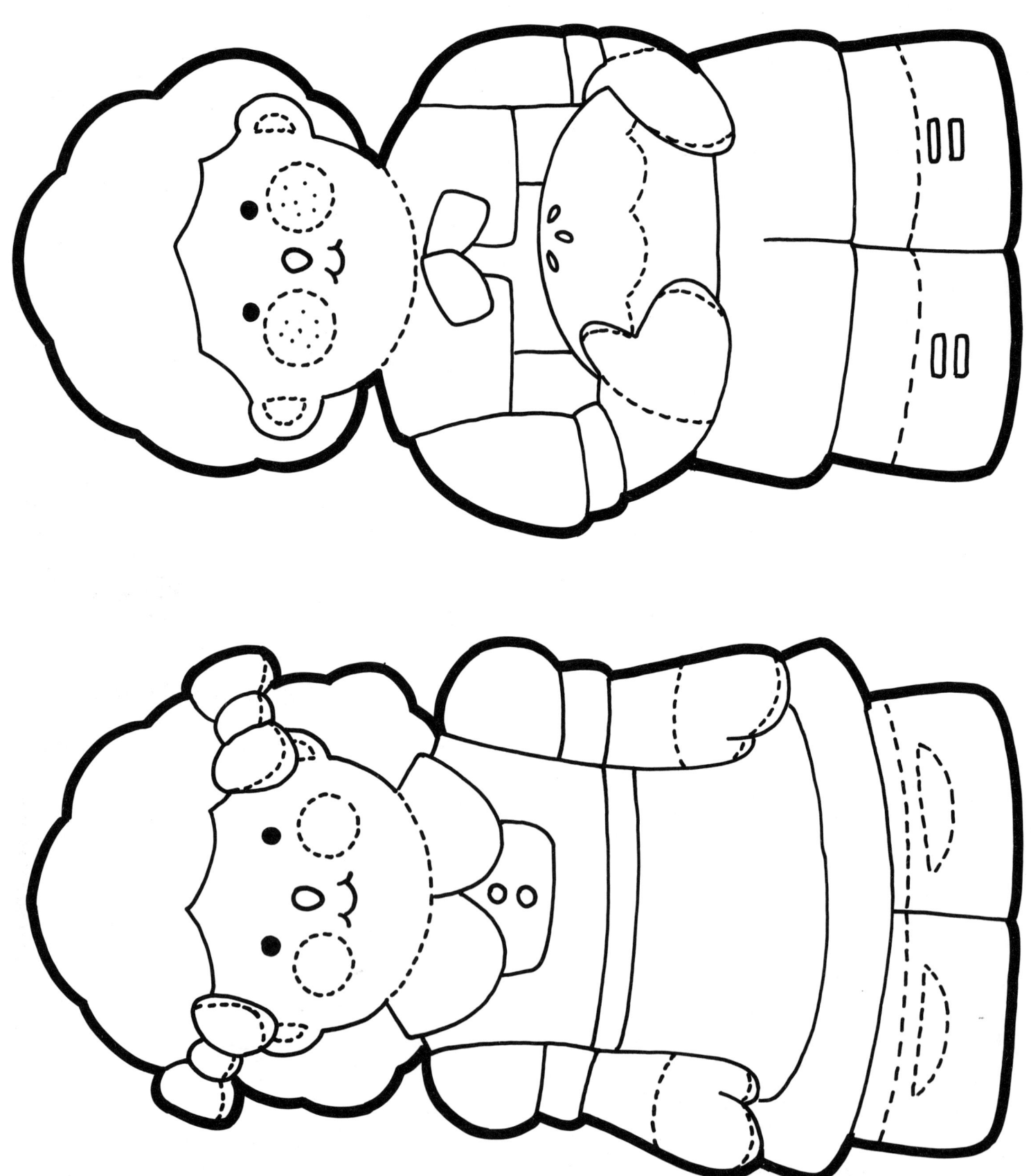

Stick Puppet Patterns
Mother Hubbard and Old King Cole

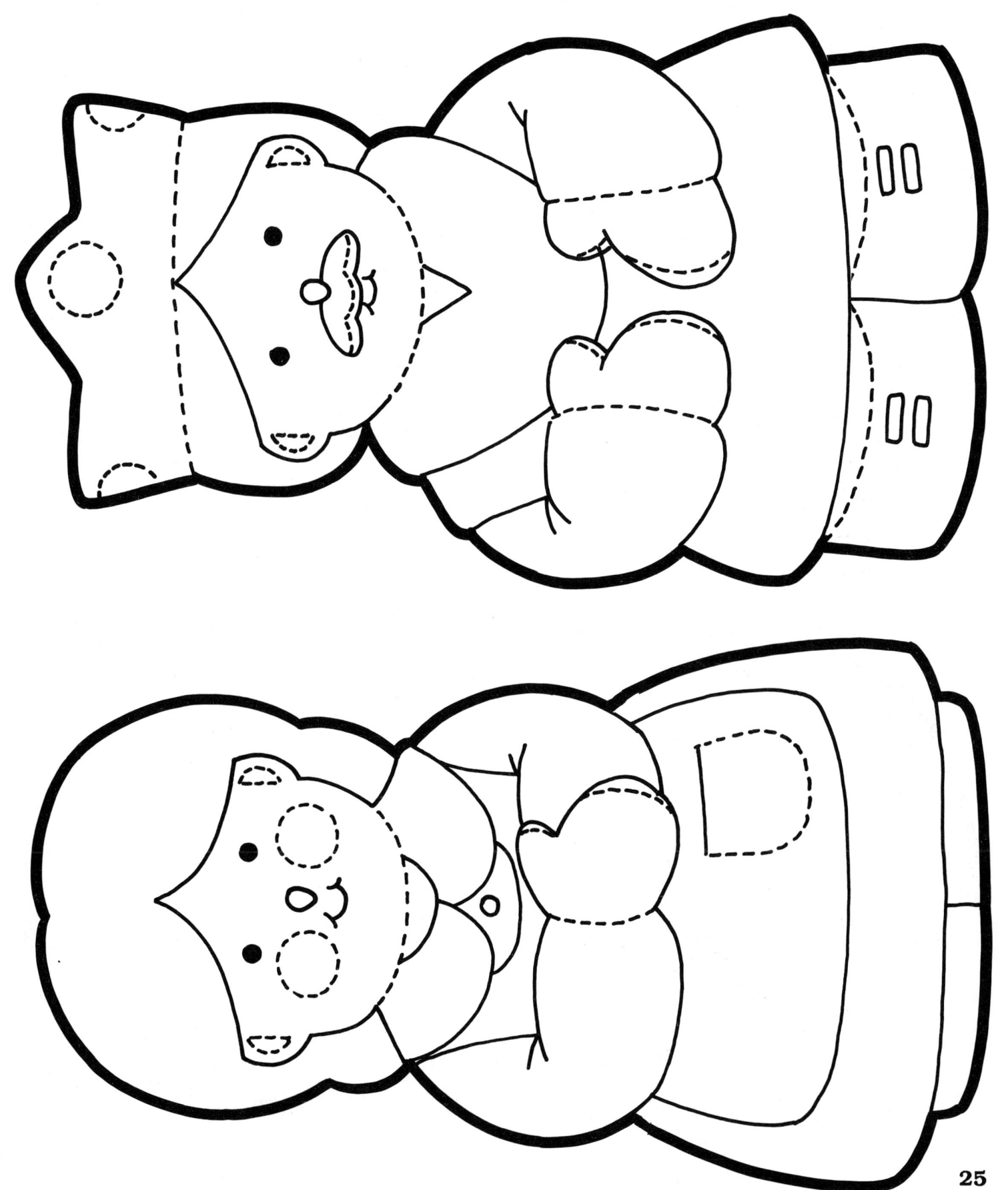

25

Stick Puppet Patterns
Moon, Dish, Spoon

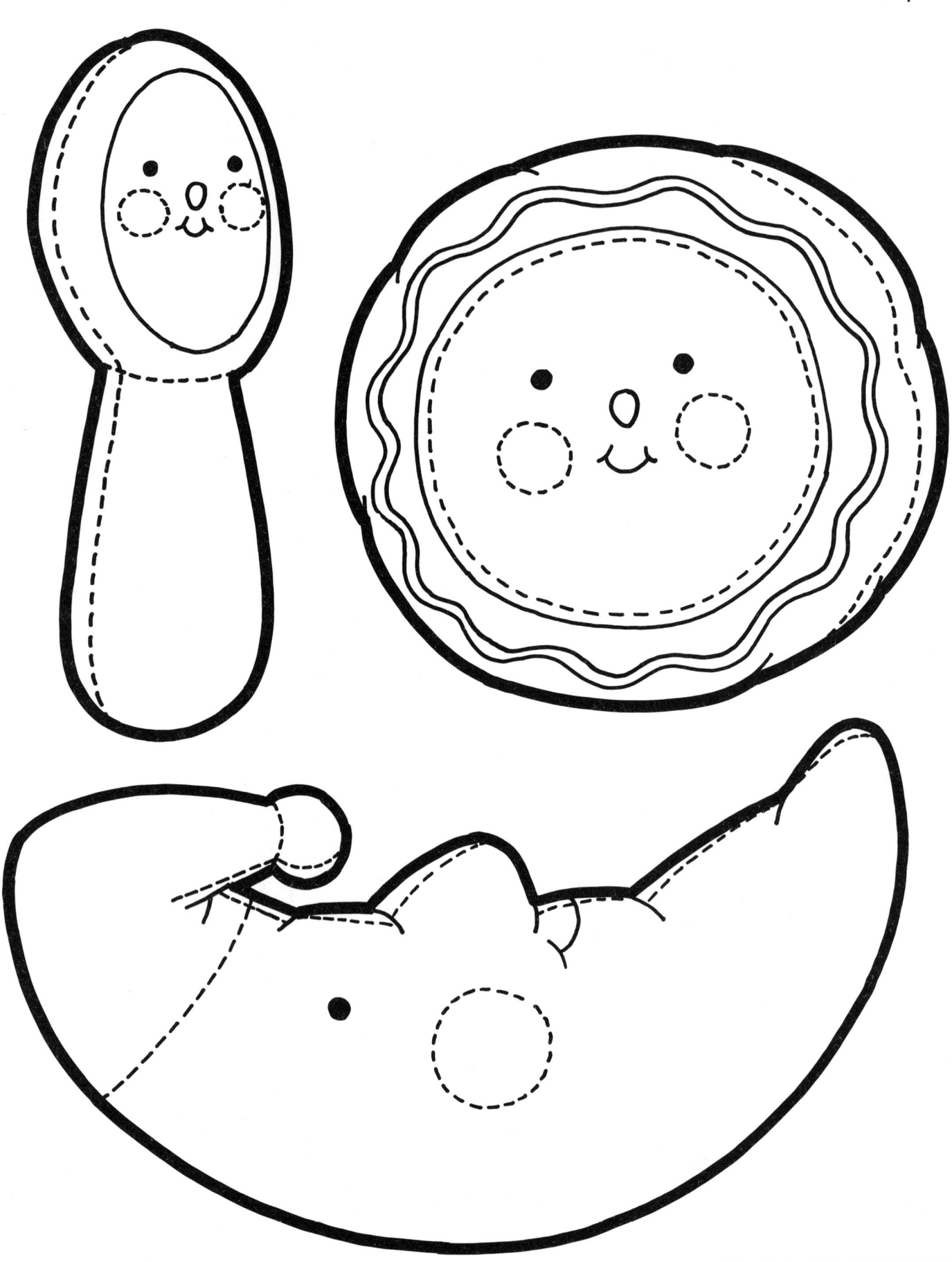

26

Stick Puppet Patterns
Bottle of Bubbles and Pipe

Stick Puppet Patterns
Bowl, Fiddle, and Spider

Stick Puppet Patterns
Caucasian Children

Stick Puppet Patterns
African American Children

Stick Puppet Patterns
Asian American Children

31

Name Tags
School Bell

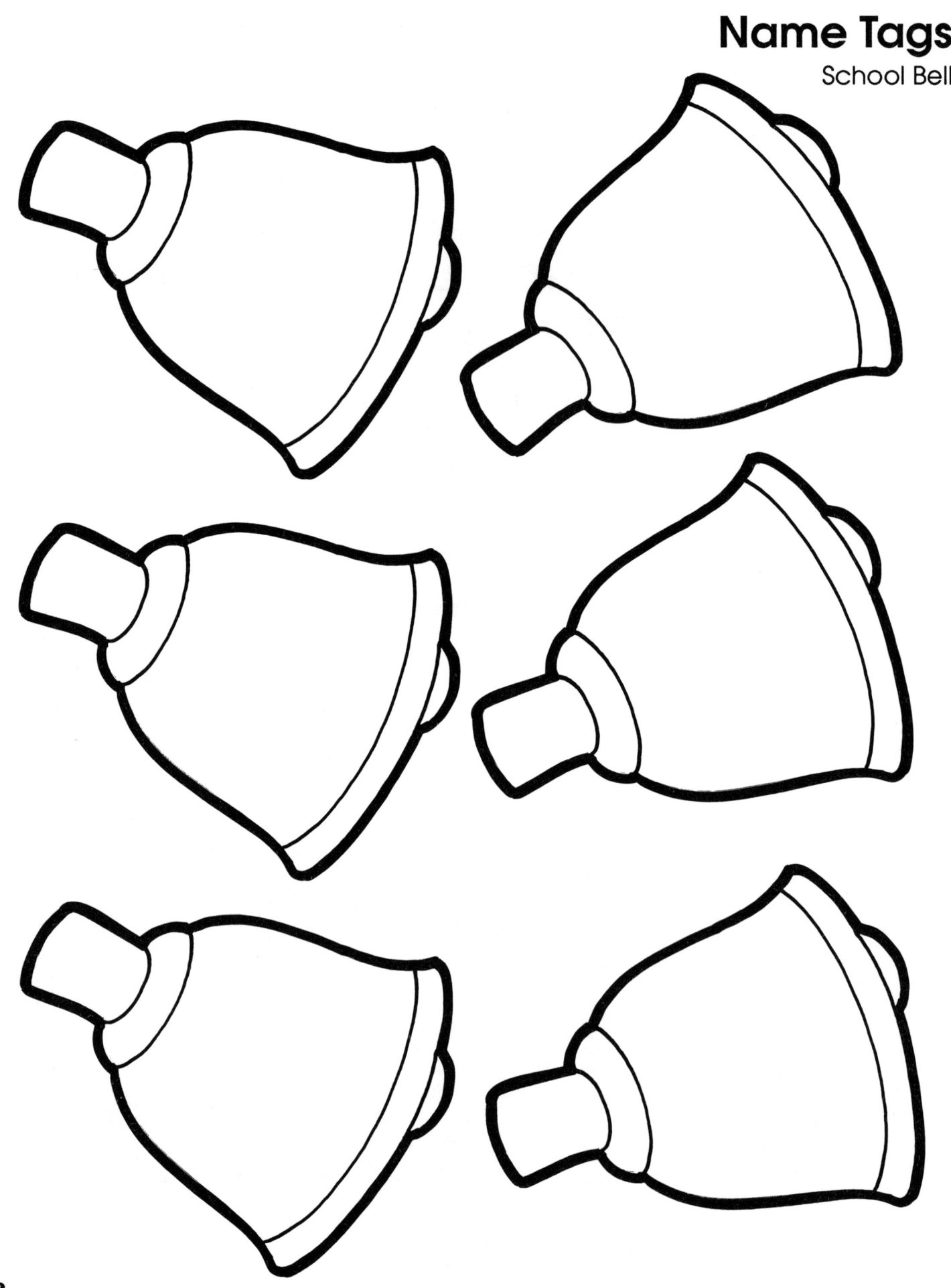

32

Name Tags
Heart

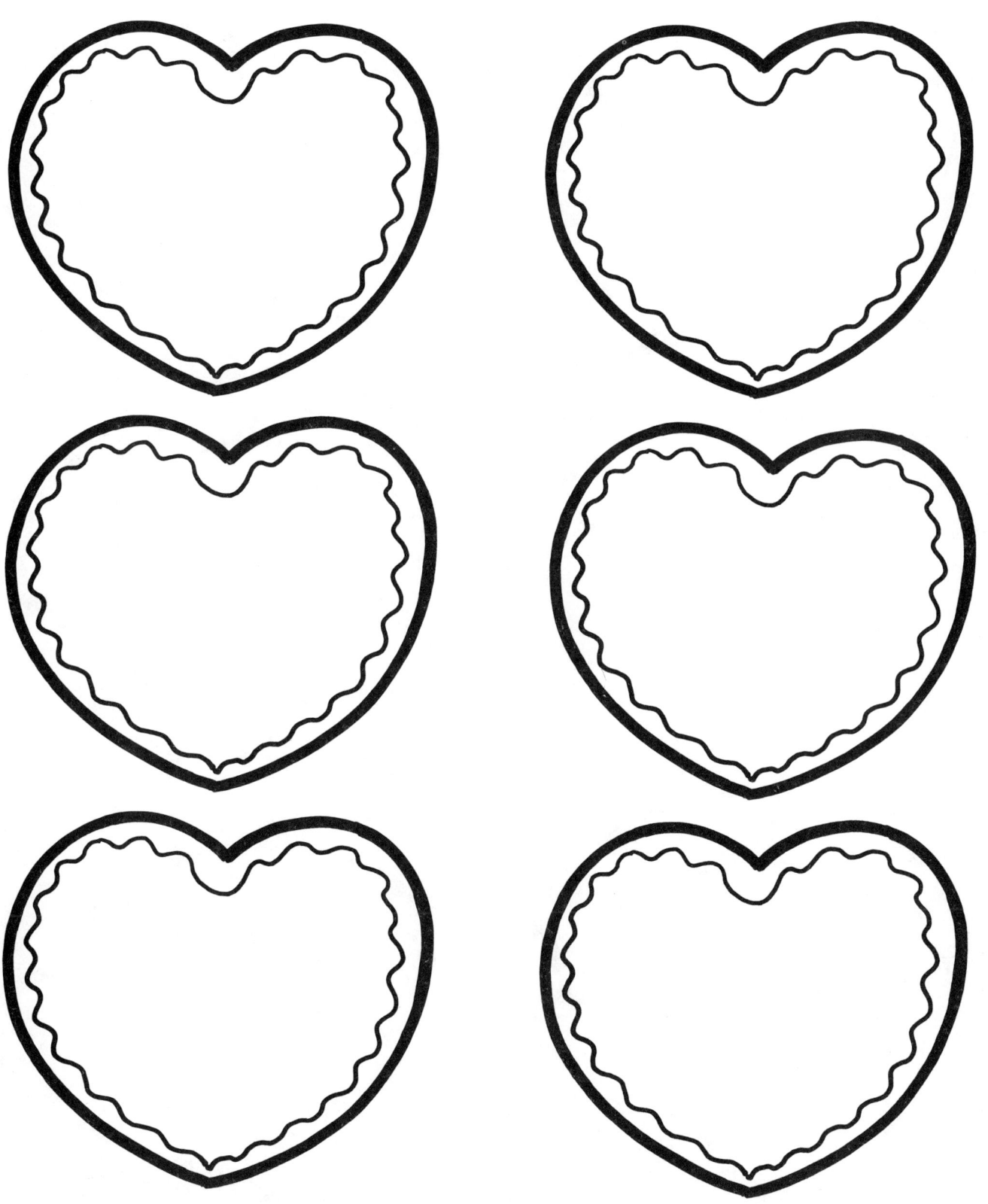

33

Name Tags
Rainbow

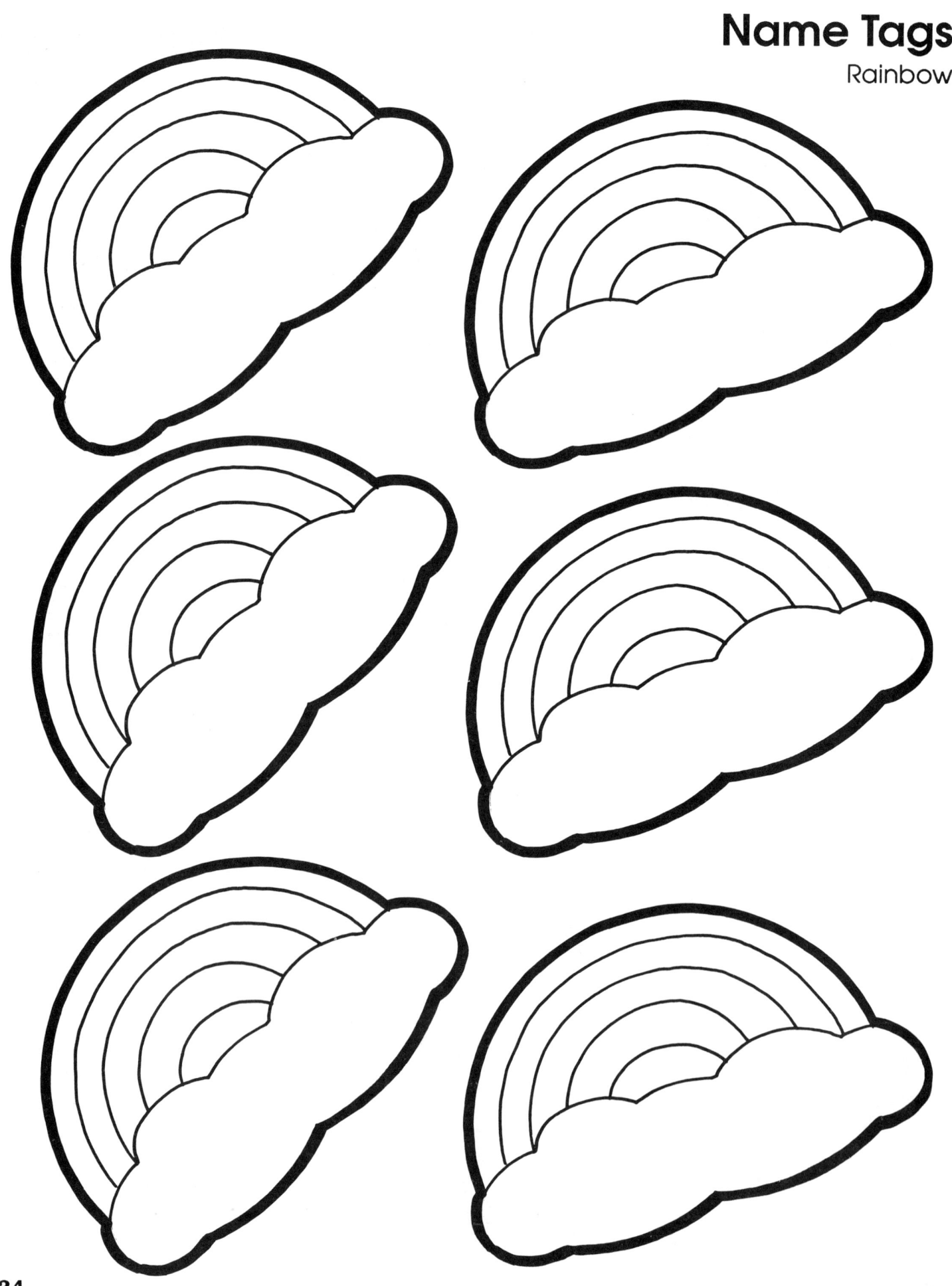

34

Name Tags
Bunny

Name Tags
Field Trip

Badges
I Can Tie!

37

Badges
I Can Lace!

Badges
I Can Count to 10

Badges
I Can...

Cubby Hole Labels
Fall

41

Cubby Hole Labels
Winter

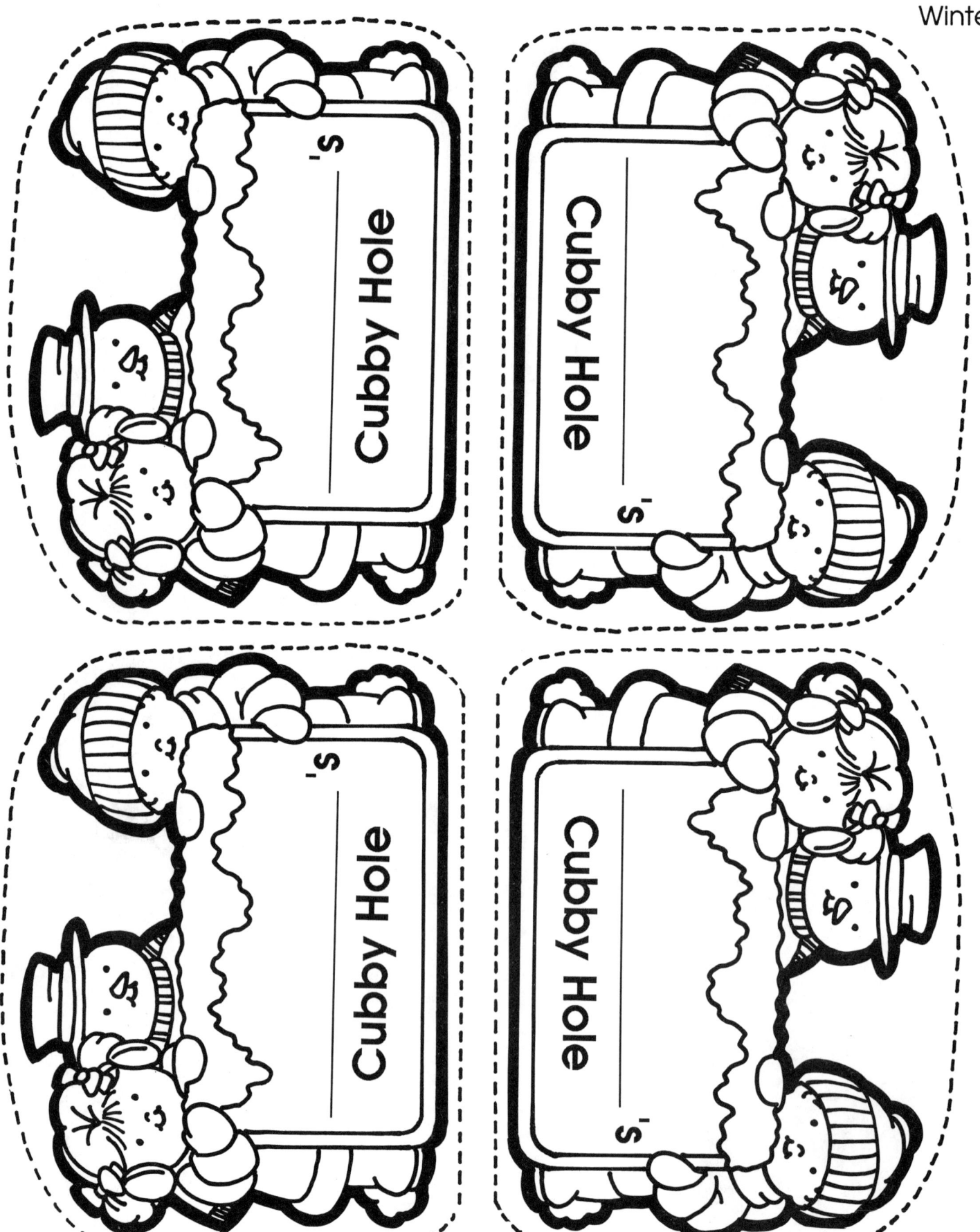

42

Cubby Hole Labels
Spring

43

Cubby Hole Labels
Summer

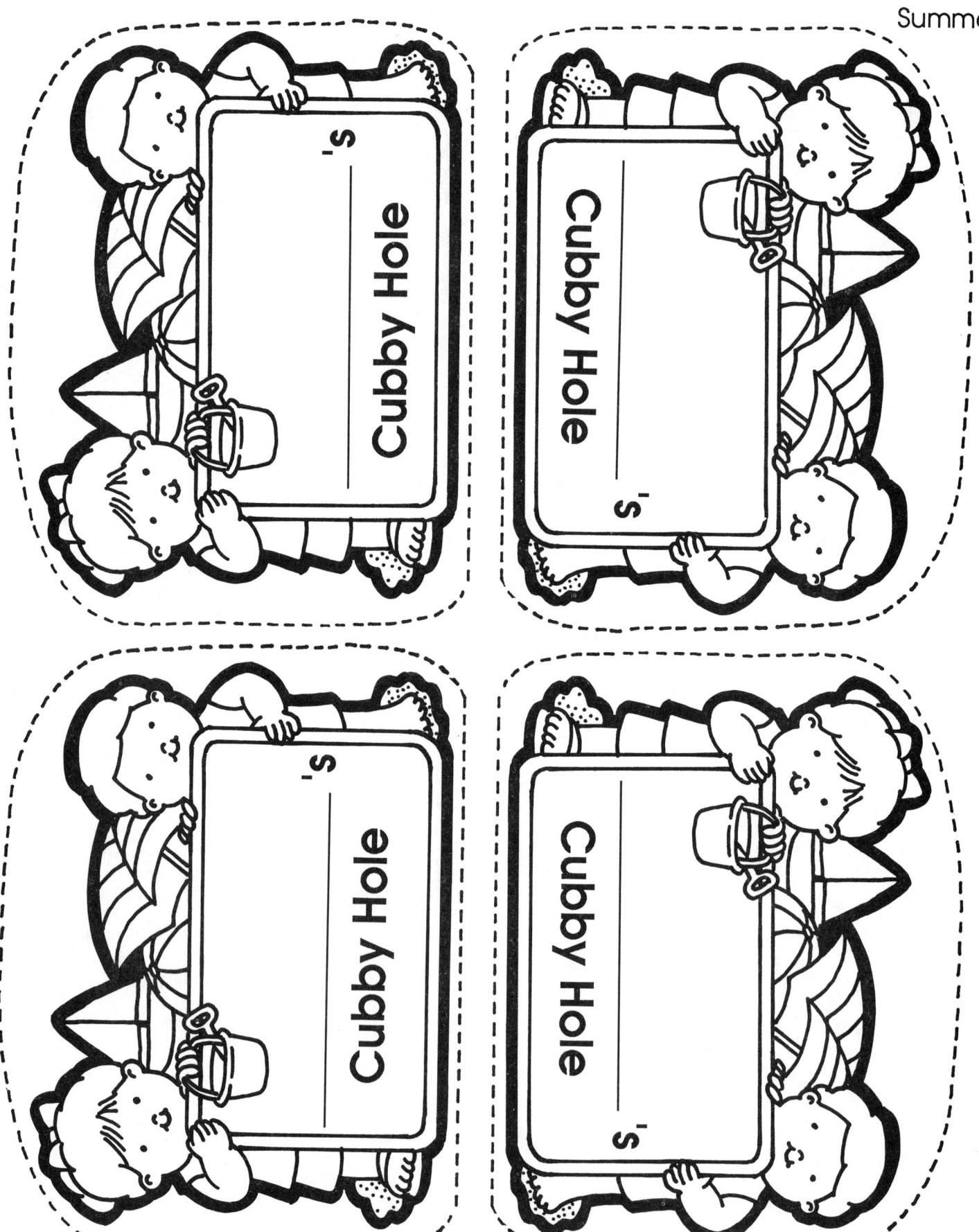

Desk Labels
Fall

_____'s

Desk

Desk

_____'s

45

Desk Labels
Winter

Desk Labels
Spring

47

Desk Labels
Summer

48

Activity Center Labels
Music

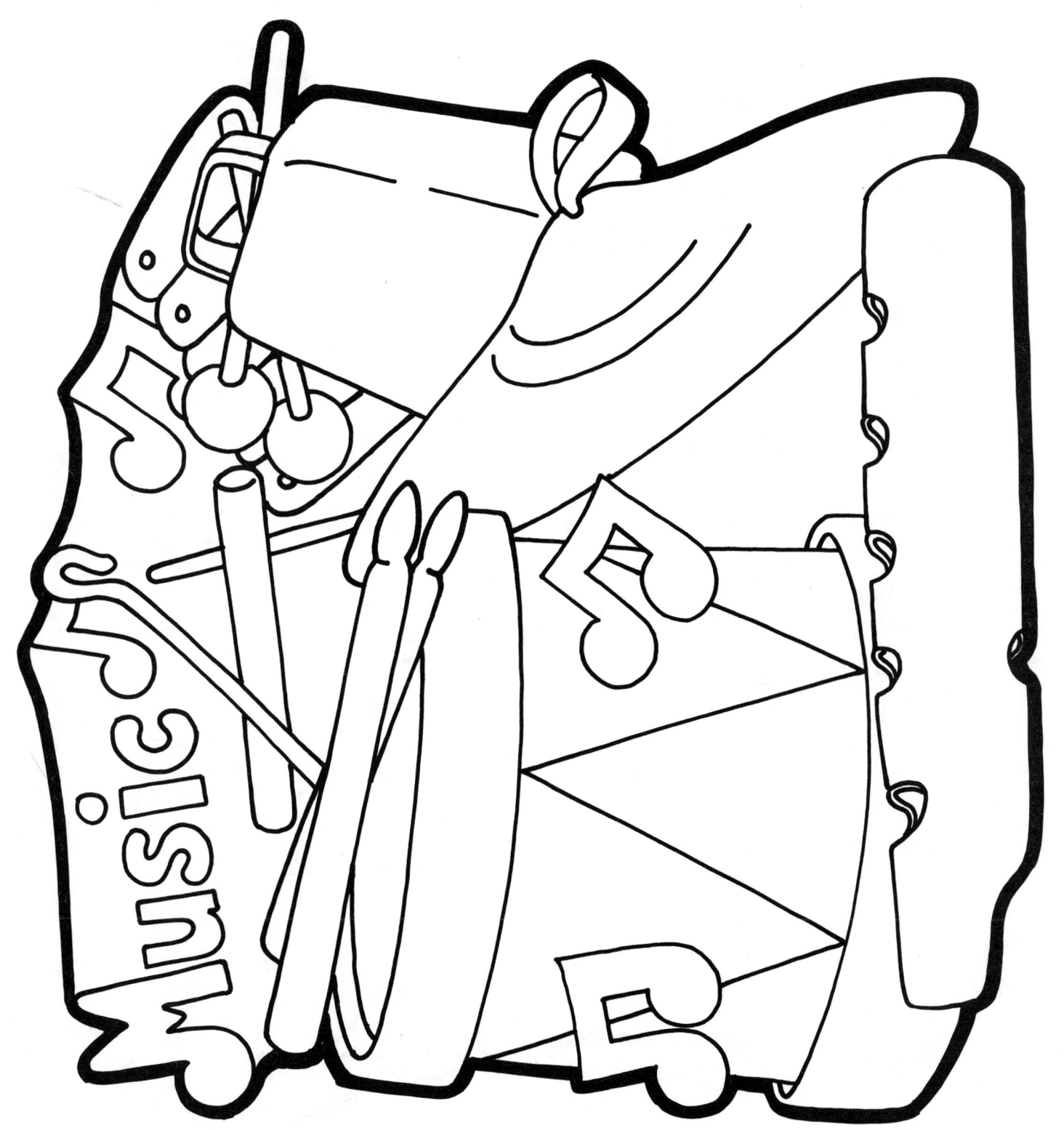

49

Activity Center Labels
Traffic Safety

50

Activity Center Labels
Reading

51

Activity Center Labels
Arts and Crafts

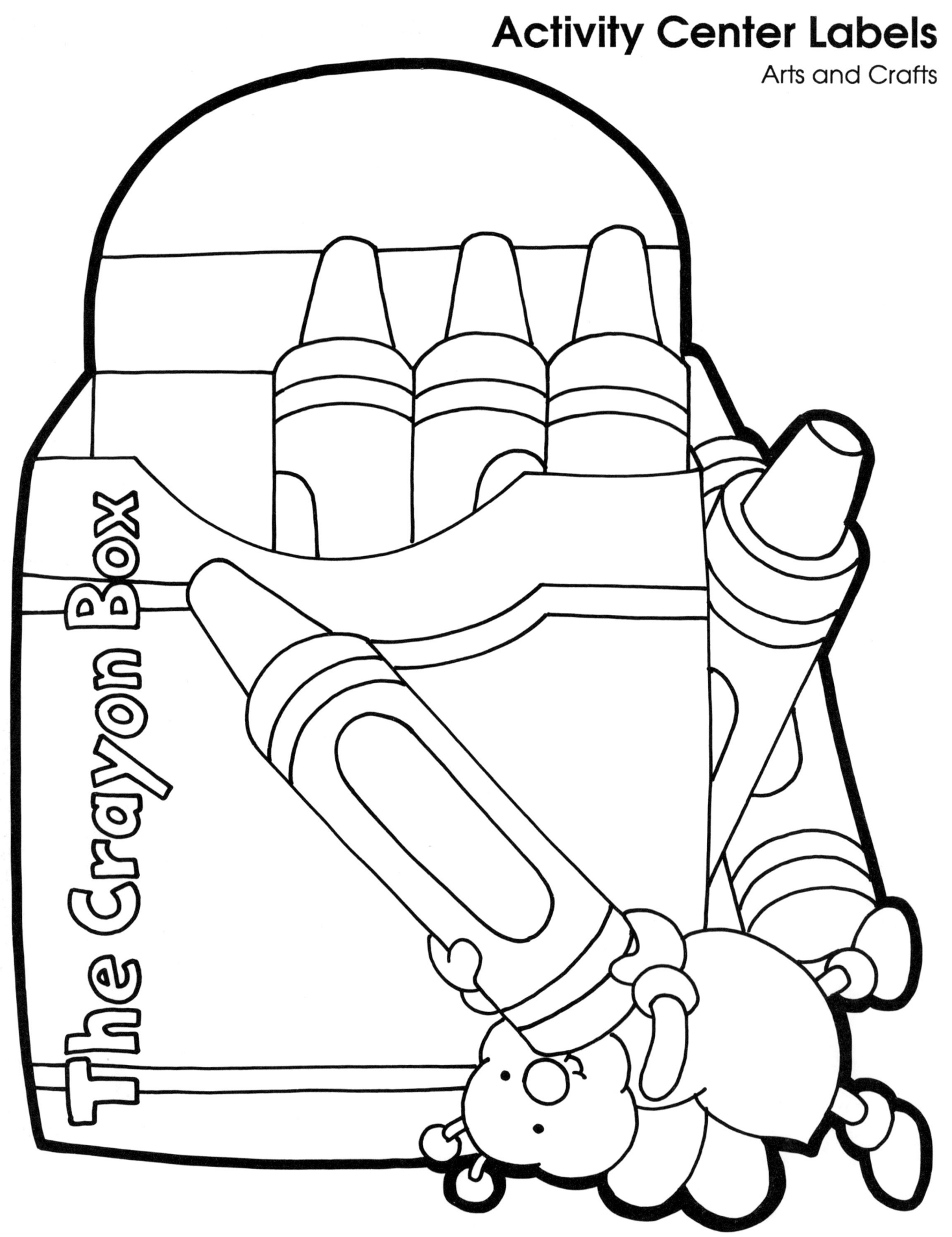

52

Activity Center Labels
Building Blocks

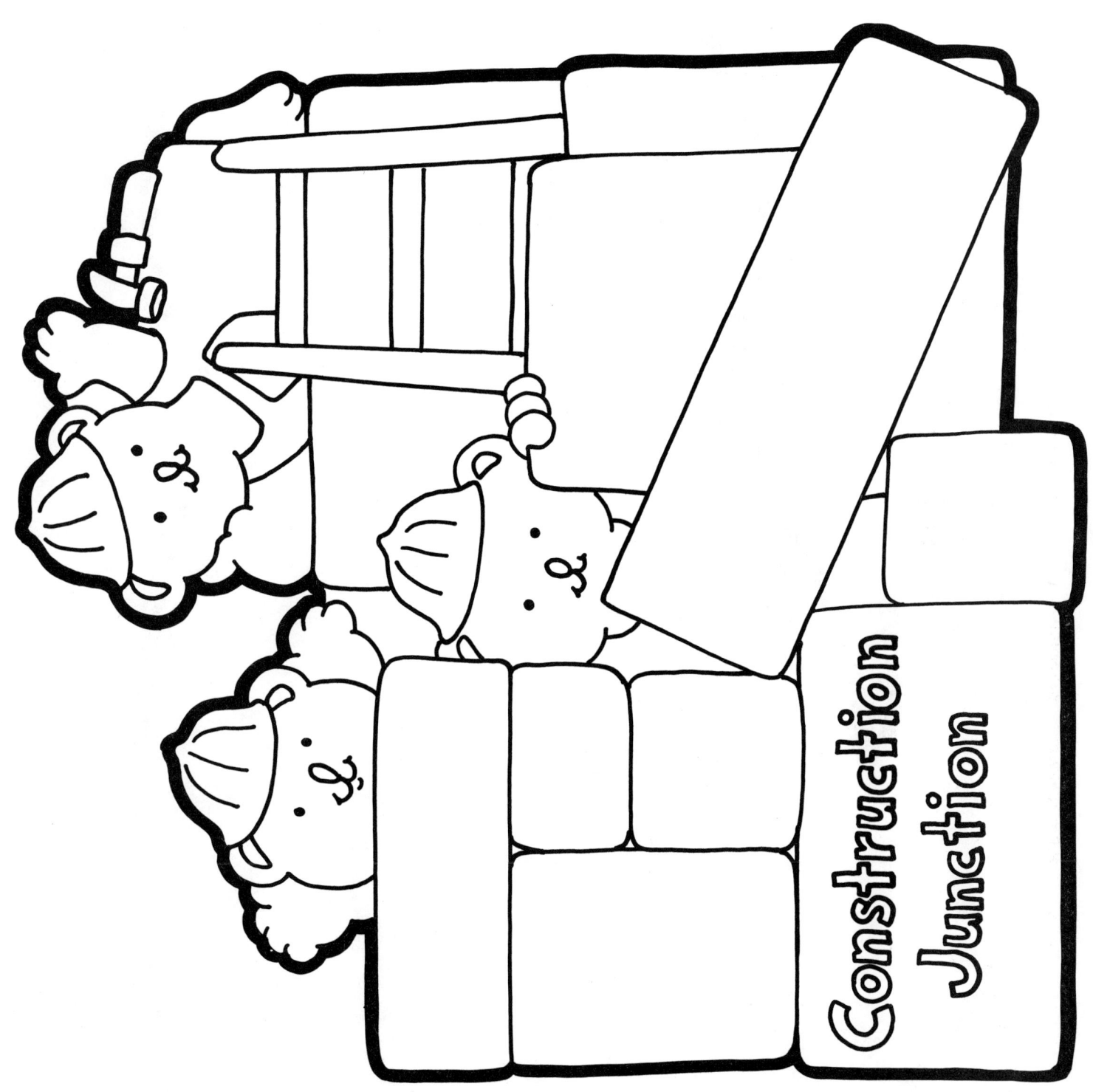

53

Outline Activity Patterns
Cat

Outline Activity Patterns
Dog

Outline Activity Patterns
Elephant

Outline Activity Patterns
Hippopotamus

Outline Activity Patterns
Pig

Outline Activity Patterns
Snail

59

Outline Activity Patterns
Teddy Bear

Outline Activity Patterns
Turtle

Outline Activity Patterns
Acorn

Outline Activity Patterns
Snowflake

Outline Activity Patterns
Umbrella

Outline Activity Patterns
Sailboat

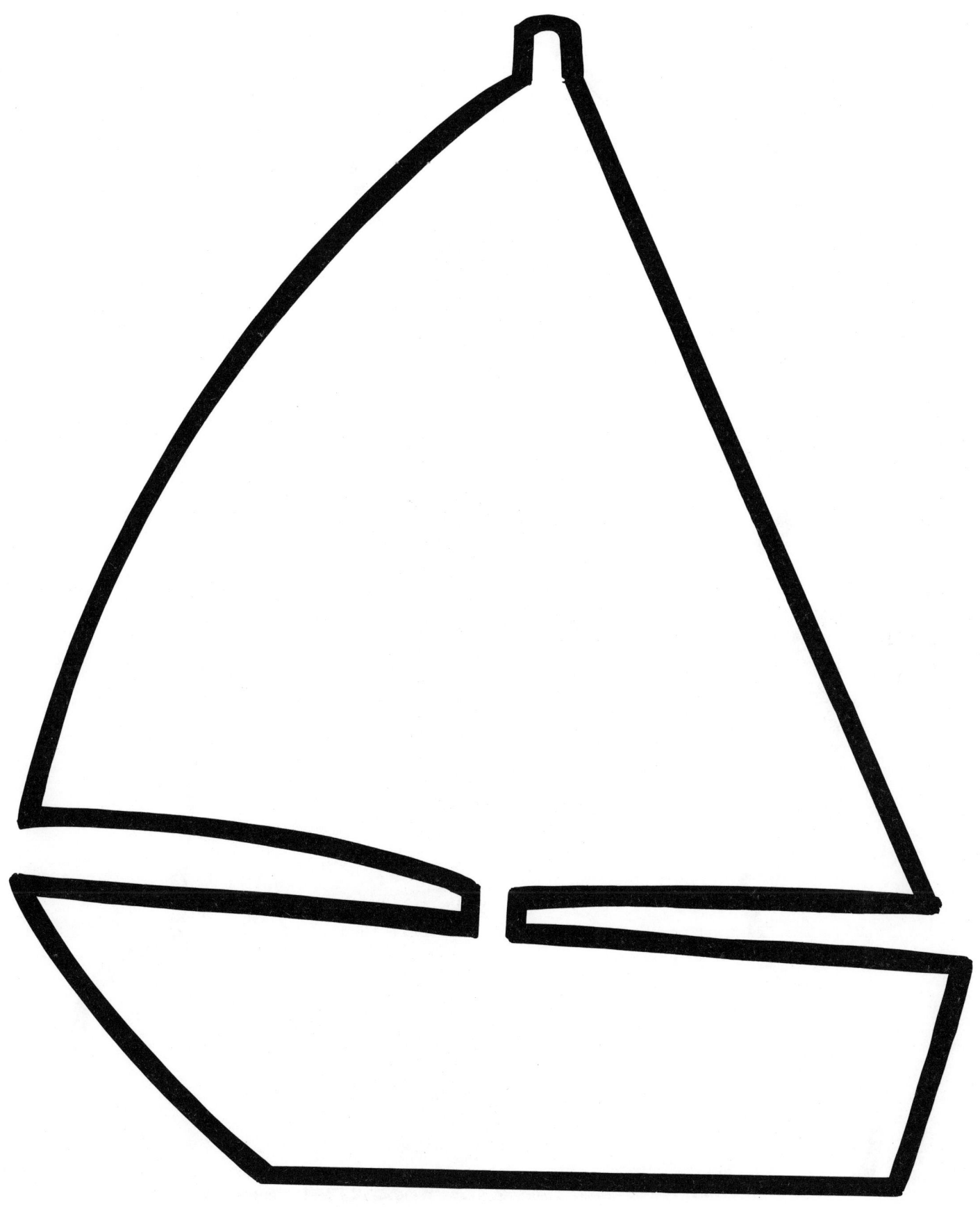

Outline Holiday Patterns
Bunny

Outline Holiday Patterns
Basket

Outline Holiday Patterns
Heart

Outline Holiday Patterns
Pumpkin

Outline Holiday Patterns
Ghost

Outline Holiday Patterns
Turkey

Outline Holiday Patterns
Stocking

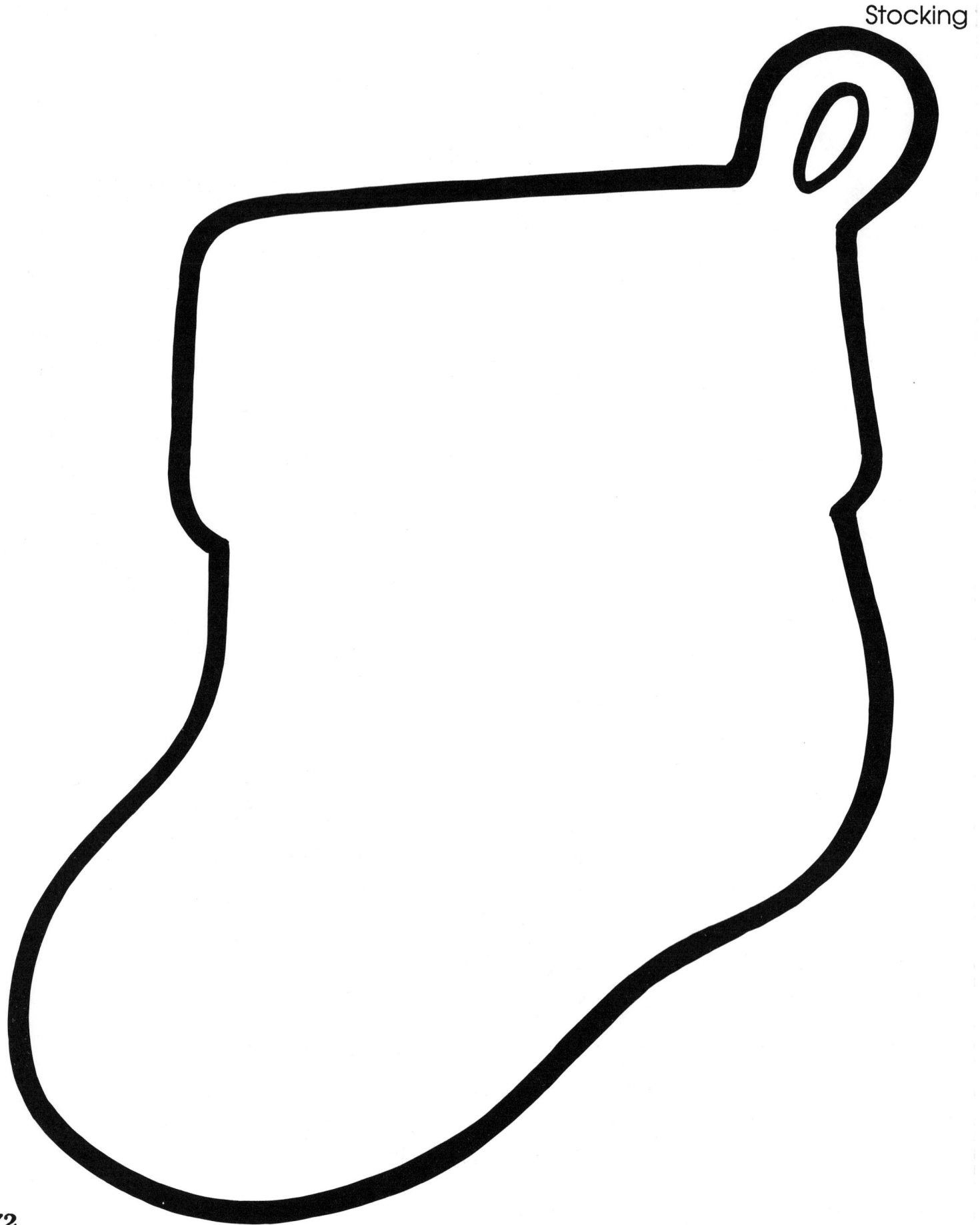

Outline Holiday Patterns
Menorah

73

Birthday Patterns
Name Tags

Birthday Patterns
Candles

75

Birthday Patterns
Headband Strips

76

Birthday Patterns
Attendance Tags

77

Attendance Tags
Snowman and Hat

Attendance Tags
Basket and Egg

79

Attendance Tags
Flowerpot and Flower

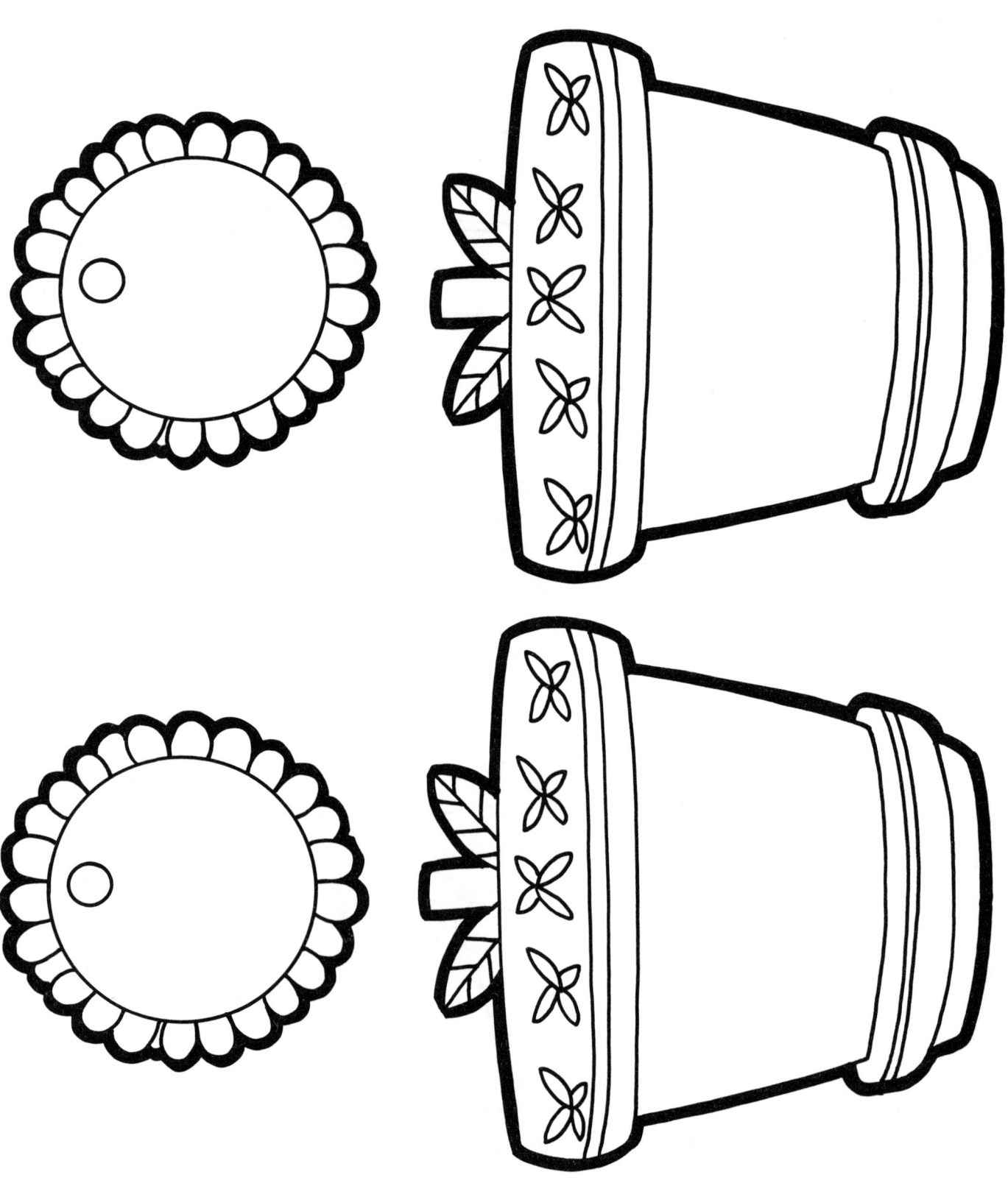

80

Attendance Tags
Teddy Bear and Bow Tie

81

Doorknob Hangers
Gone for a Walk

82

Doorknob Hangers
Gone to the Library

Doorknob Hangers
Gone on a Field Trip

Gone on a field trip.

Doorknob Hanger
Resting

85

Doorknob Hangers
We're Having a Party

MONTH

Calendars
Open Teacher Calendar

MONTH

87

Calendars
Open Student Calendar

Monday	**Tuesday**	**Wednesday**	**Thursday**

Calendars
Open Student Calendar

Friday	Saturday	Sunday

Calendars
Calendar Cap - January

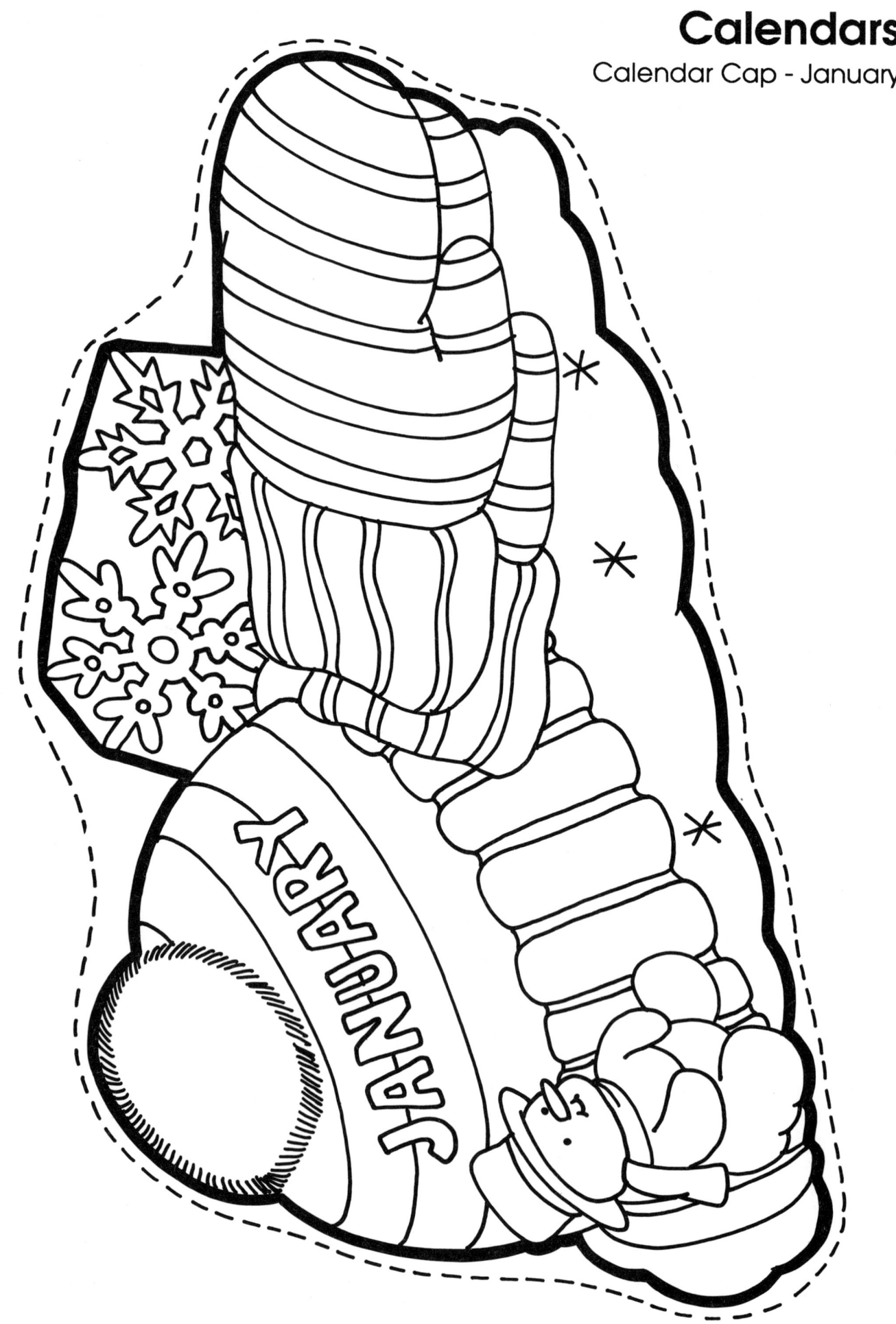

90

Calendars
Calendar Cap - February

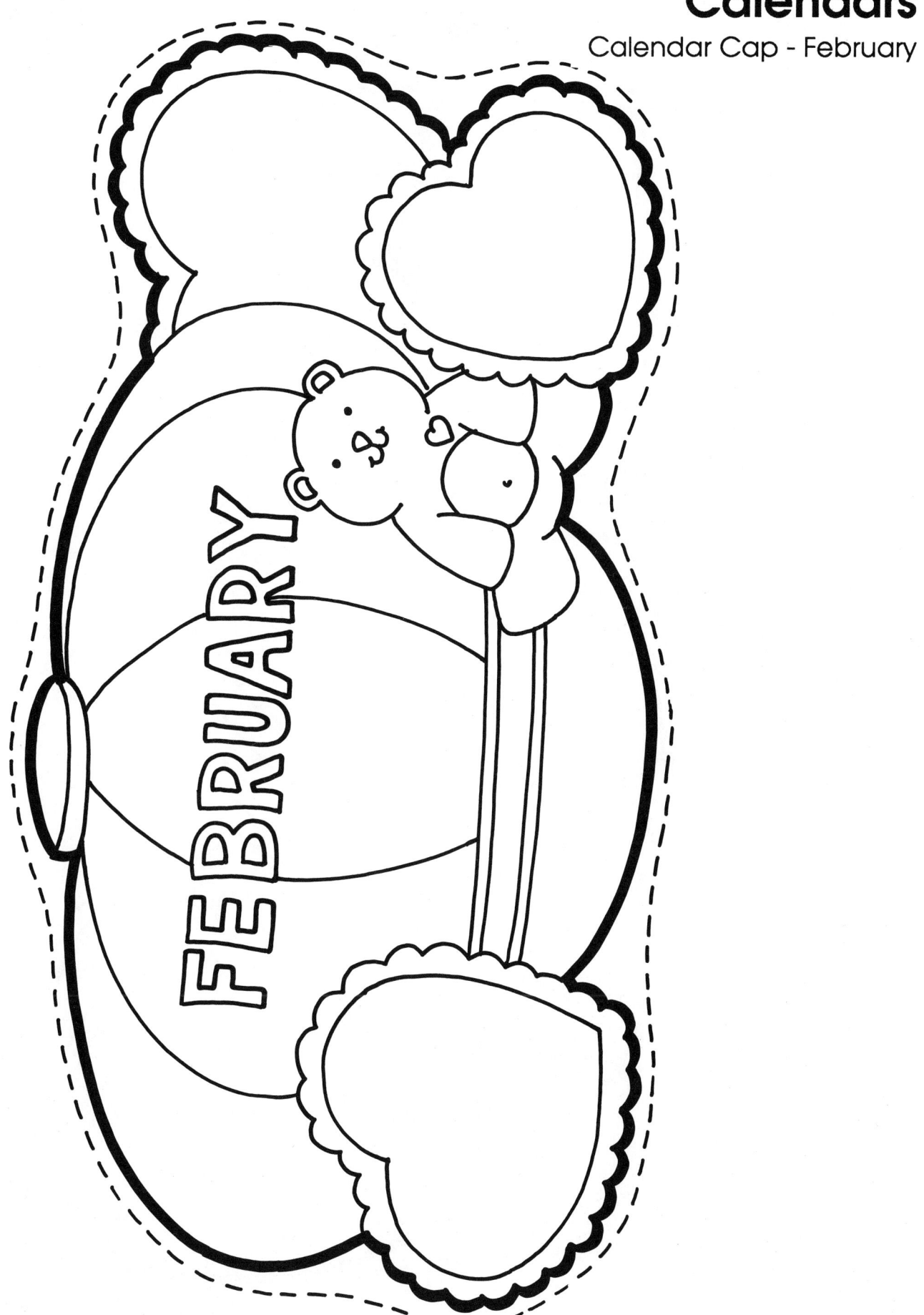

91

Calendars
Calendar Cap - March

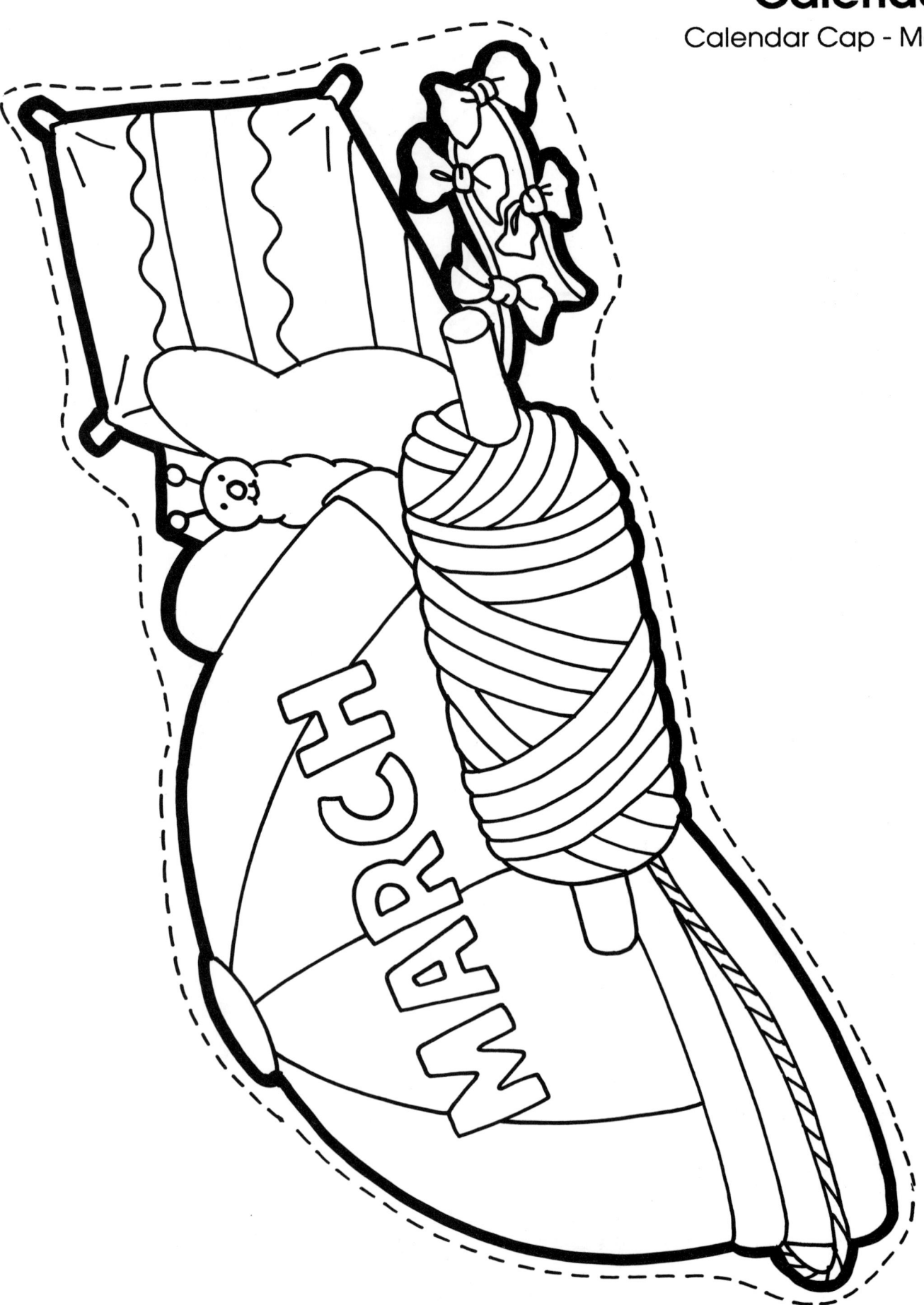

92

Calendars
Calendar Cap - April

93

Calendars
Calendar Cap - May

94

Calendars
Calendar Cap - June

95

Calendars
Calendar Cap - July

Calendars
Calendar Cap - August

97

Calendars
Calendar Cap - September

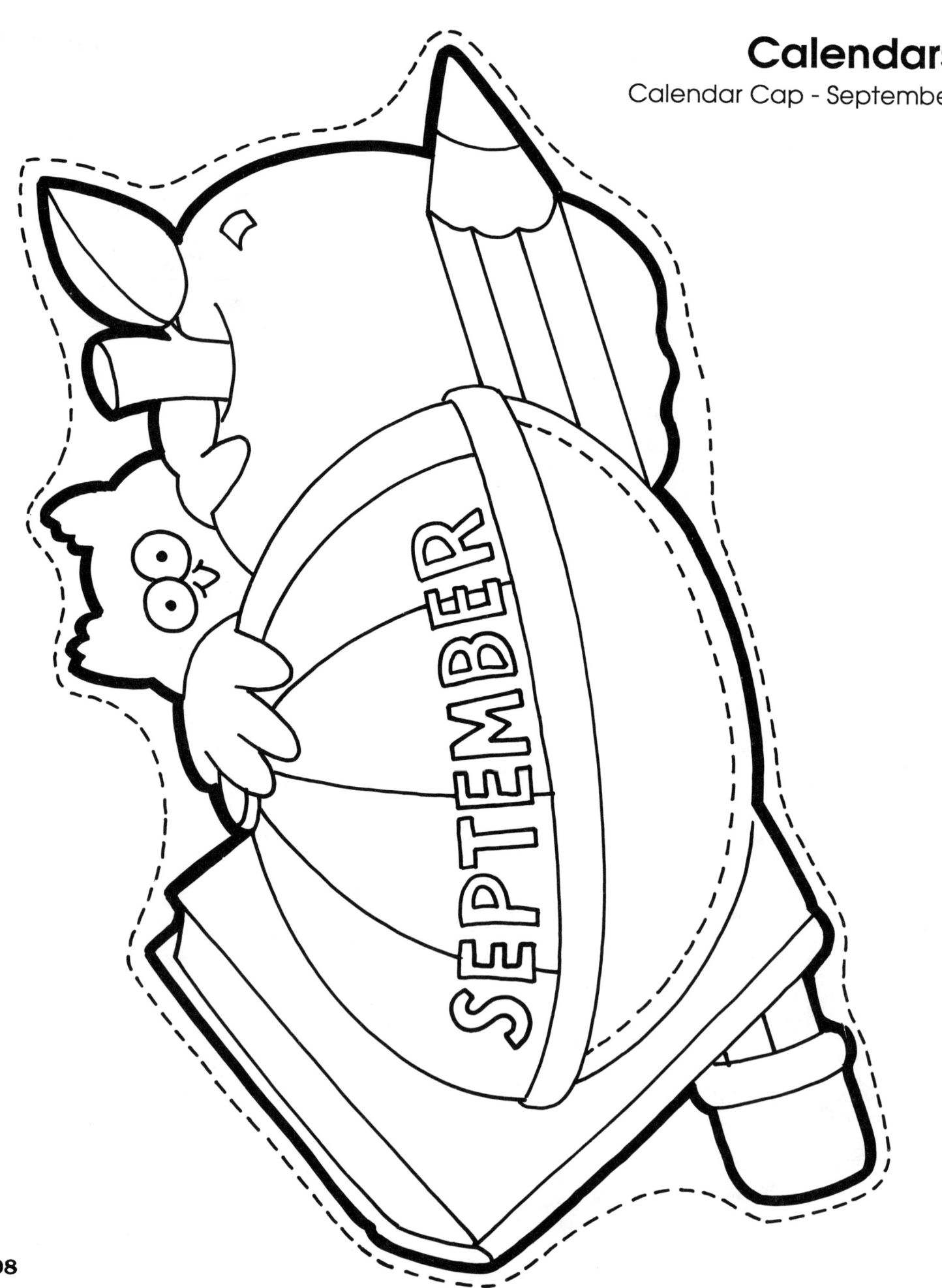

Calendars
Calendar Cap - October

Calendars
Calendar Cap - November

100

Calendars
Calendar Cap - December

101

Calendars
Student Calendar Event Stickers

Calendars
Student Calendar Weather Stickers

103

Activity Poster
Let's Go Shopping!

Activity Poster
What's Cooking?

Activity Poster
When I Grow Up. . .

Clips Collection
Fall

107

Clips Collection
Fall

Clips Collection
Fall

109

Clips Collection
Winter

My Wish List

110

Clips Collection
Winter

111

Clips Collection
Winter

Clips Collection
Spring

113

Clips Collection
Spring

114

Clips Collection
Spring

115

Clips Collection
Summer

Clips Collection
Summer

Clips Collection
Summer

Let's Play Dress Up
Astronaut

119

Let's Play Dress Up
Farmer

Let's Play Dress Up
Magician

121

Teacher Note
Take-Home Award

1 2 3 4 5 6 7 8 9 10

_____

knows his/her

Numbers

Hooray!

_____ _____
Date   Teacher

Teacher Note
Take-Home Award

_____ knows his/her **Colors**

Congratulations!

Date — Teacher

123

Teacher Note
Take-Home Award

Teacher Note
Take-Home Award

A B C D E F G H I J K L M N O P

_____

knows his/her

Alphabet

Great!

_____ _____
Date   Teacher

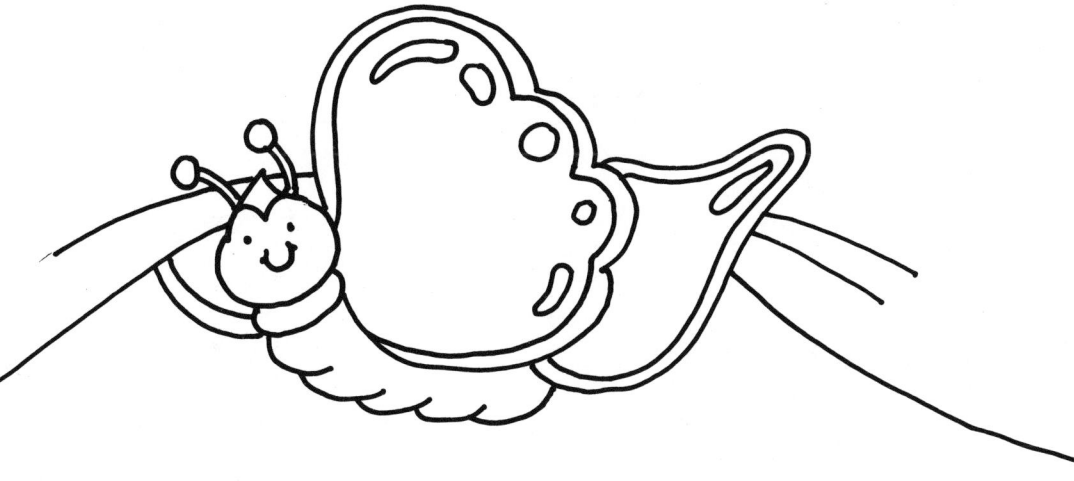

Q R S T U V W X Y Z

125

Teacher Note
Take-Home Letter

We are learning

about _____

_____

_____

_____

_____

_____

_____   _____
Date   Teacher

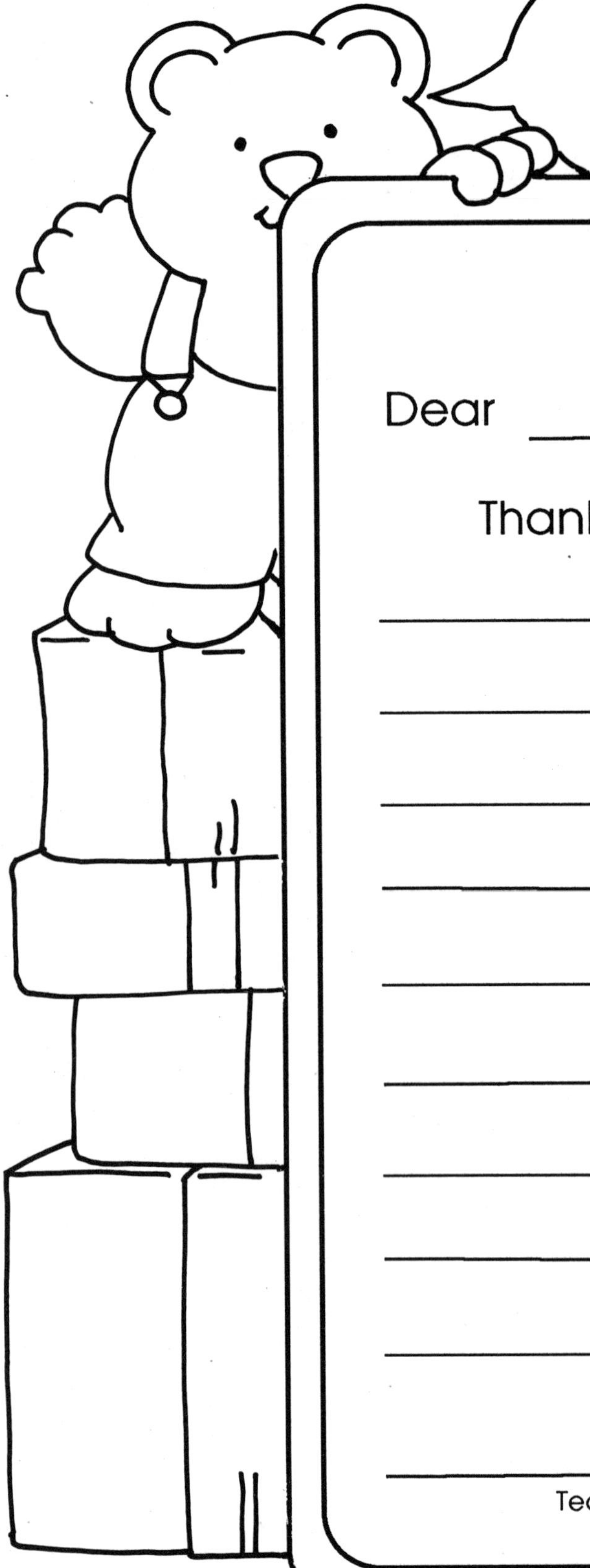

Teacher Note
Take-Home Letter

Thank you very much!

Dear _____,

Thank you for _____

_____

_____

_____

_____

_____

_____

_____

_____

_____
Teacher